CULTS

THE CORNERSTONE
CHRISTIAN FELLOWSHIP

Lowell D. Streiker

ABINGDON PRESS
Nashville

CULTS
A Festival Book

Copyright © 1978, 1983 by Lowell D. Streiker

All rights reserved

Festival edition published February 1983

ISBN 0-687-10069-0
(Previously titled *The Cults Are Coming!* published also by Abingdon under ISBN 0-687-10070-4)

Photograph on p. 26 is from *Sun Myung Moon and the Unification Church* by Frederick Sontag. © 1977 by Abingdon

Printed in the United States of America

CONTENTS

I. The Cults Are Coming!.................7
II. The Unification Church of Sun Myung Moon 20
III. The Children of God....................50
IV. Hare Krishna!........................... 67
V. Is All This Really Necessary?.......... 96
VI. Group Leaders, Greed, and Coercion......... 110
VII. What Can We Do?...................119
VIII. The Peoples Temple and Jonestown........... 125
IX. Freedom Counseling Center—
    An Innovative Approach...................... 134
    Notes................................. 145

To Connie

I. THE CULTS ARE COMING!

The cults are coming—to your city—to your neighborhood—to the family next door—to your family—to your life!

An invasion is under way. Beachheads have already been established in communities throughout America. Strange ideas, exotic practices, peculiar attitudes, unfamiliar mode of speech—these are some characteristics of the invaders.

Some observers welcome the newcomers as harbingers of an age of utopia, prophets of a new consciousness, guides to paths of stress-free righteousness, allies in the cause of preserving all that our society once held precious. Numerous writers, scholars, and public figures encourage us to heed the voices of these "strangers at the door," "new believers," "new gods in America," "new religions." The governor of the most populous state in the nation not only finds personal solace at a Zen retreat center, but he invites the saffron-robed devotees of Krishna and representatives of the Church of Scientology to provide volunteers for a state-sponsored program of patient visitation in mental hospitals.

Others view the manifestations of the new religious consciousness with fear, suspicion, and loathing. Converts have been kidnapped, held against their will, and remorselessly pressured into renouncing their beliefs. Such deprogramming is not only tolerated in a society based upon principles of free religious expression; in some instances, it has been ordered by the courts.

The cults are coming. The advocates of all manner of spiritual disciplines are at the door. They are in our midst. Exaggerated depictions of their practices and powers fill popular literature, motion picture screens, newspapers, and television. *Rosemary's Baby, The Exorcist, The Omen, Carrie,* and the like appeal to our deepest sense of dread, our gut feeling that something is wrong with our world and that we are menaced by forces beyond ourselves—malevolent, capricious, and vicious forces.

The cults are here. Some of our friends, our friends' children, our own children, have been estranged from us by the Children of God or the Hare Krishnas or the Moonies or the self-proclaimed savior-gods from the Orient. Many of us are involved in what we consider harmless flirtations with astrology, transcendental meditation, and spiritualism. Most of us would never forsake our spiritual heritage or way of life for a weird religious fringe group any more than we would give up our job and social identity to live by our wits and exertions in the wilds of some distant land. But aren't we attracted somehow by every new promise of peace of mind, of emotional closeness to other human beings, of a future filled with hope and fulfillment?

What Is a Cult?

What is a cult? Why does it arise? What needs does it satisfy?

A cult is a movement of social protest and personal affirmation. It offers a total way of life to those who are alienated from their families and the attitudes by which their families and their society attempted to prepare them for successful adulthood. Cults attract the dispossessed, the bored, the lonely. Neither poverty nor youth is a necessary precondition for feeling the lure of a cult.

The tenets of a cult are set forth by a founder-prophet. Cult members are highly dependent upon their leader —even if they have never seen him. Cults are not founded (as are other small sects) upon appeals "to the classical, the primitive, the 'true' interpretation of the dominant religion." [1] They are exotic novelties of religious expression within a given society. They claim to embody the essence of a particular ancient tradition, but essentially they represent a definite break with prevailing religions.

For example, the Children of God was originally a Fundamentalist-Pentecostal sect dedicated to proclaiming and living by the most literal interpretation of the Bible. However, in recent years the importance of the Bible as the only source of guidance for doctrine or practice has been supplanted by writings of the enigmatic founder-prophet Moses David.

Krishna Consciousness is a manifestation of traditional Hinduism, which is the major religion of India. But Krishna's devotees are not Indians. In the Western world—on the streets of New York, for instance—Krishna

Consciousness is a social anomaly and a religious novelty.

Cults flourish in an atmosphere of stress and rapid social change. When daily existence is experienced as heroic struggle as it was during the last World War, when one's very life is on the line for the sake of traditional social values, when national leadership commands total devotion—at such times, cults serve few needs. But if life is too easy, if the individual has neither purpose nor direction, if there is no ordeal ahead to test courage and ideals—at these times, cults are indispensable.

Give a man a fish and you feed him for a day. Teach a man to fish and you feed him for a lifetime. Give a man a life's supply of fish and you destroy him. The hunger that drives men and women toward novel, difficult, self-abnegating paths is seldom born of economic need. On the contrary, a hallmark of the cults is their repudiation of the competitive, acquisitive materialism of our society. (They do not always escape the "root of all evil" as we shall see.) The ways of the cults are demanding and difficult. They are not for the careless, the lazy, the fainthearted, the sunshine disciple, or the part-time enthusiast. The rolls of cult membership are made up of seekers and drifters, the intelligent and the confused, the sincere and the hypocritical, as are all human endeavors. But the cults impose harsh standards of discipline. It is not enough for you to choose them; they must also accept you. And you must merit your membership by wholehearted devotion. If you fail, you will be disciplined or expelled. If you remain, you will know that you belong to the chosen, the elite, those set apart from ordinary mortals. You will be accepted as a member of a new family, as an individual having worth and dignity within the group. You will attain status, knowledge, and power over your destiny. In place of aimless self-indulgence you will learn self-control. Instead of self-hatred and depression you will gain self-respect and a sense of purpose. Where there was inner confusion there will be transcendent authority that cannot be doubted.[2]

The appearance is that cults produce dropouts. They certainly attract those who simply cannot fit in with demands of our society—the drug burnouts, the rejects, the jobless, the vagabonds who float from movement to movement. But after the ordeal of self-sacrifice and dedication, the convert usually internalizes standards of behavior surprisingly like those of the middle class which the convert intentionally shuns. This is not always so, but it frequently is.

The success of the current plethora of cults owes much to the media. Television and the press not only call attention to the bizarre and the unusual groups, providing them with free advertising as it were, but they throw a spotlight on every effort to suppress and restrict them.

Cults are always regarded with suspicion and hostility by the families of those from whom converts have been won. Since parents of converts are more likely to win the ears of local authorities than are the converts themselves, cults are harassed by the institutions charged with social control and conflict resolution—the courts, police, mental health services, and other public agencies. At an earlier time, mob action, lynchings, beatings, and arson were common responses to the incursion of the cults. In the two years following the 1940 Supreme Court decision that upheld the constitutionality of expelling the children of Jehovah's Witnesses from public schools for refusing to salute the flag, hundreds of acts of violence were committed against the Witnesses. As Leo Pfeffer recalls:

At Kennebunk, Maine, their Kingdom Hall was burned. At Rockville, Maryland, the police assisted a mob in dispersing a Bible meeting. At Litchfield, Illinois, practically the entire town mobbed a company of some sixty Witnesses who were canvassing it. At Connersville, Indiana, several Witnesses were charged with riotous conspiracy, their attorney mobbed, beaten and driven out of town. At Jackson, Mississippi, members of a veterans' organization forcibly removed a number of Witnesses and their trailer homes from the town. In Nebraska, a Witness was lured from his house, abducted, and castrated. In Richwood, West Virginia, the chief of police and deputy sheriff forced a group of Witnesses to drink large doses of castor oil and paraded the victims through the streets, tied together with police department rope.[3]

Barely three years later, the Supreme Court would reverse itself, ruling that children could not be barred from schools for refusing to salute the flag. But, between 1940 and 1942 the Jehovah's Witnesses were the victims of nearly uninterrupted violence and persecution. Today the go-everywhere, see-everything eyes and ears of modern mass media have tempered public reactions. The violence is now more subtle and psychological—though still very real.

The role of the founder-prophet is absolutely essential to such cults as Krishna Consciousness, the Children of God, the Unification Church, the Church of Scientology, the Divine Light Mission, the Church of Satan, and dozens of other groups. For the potential adherents of small religious movements are not only looking for something but someone to believe in. Theological and scriptural statements are relatively easy to interpret, compare, criticize, and reject. But persons are mysteries that can never be totally comprehended. Ultimately we will have to approach the founder-prophet if we are to deal with the essence of the cult. And this is a terribly delicate business. For when we are considering an individual such as Maharaj Ji or Moses David or Prabhupada or Sun Myung Moon, his function as founder-prophet is actually much more significant than his person (traits, history, opinions, etc.). It is the faith of the followers—the reverence and worship that the disciples have invested in their leader—that transforms the man into an object of veneration.

To worship a human being, to treat him as a god, to find freedom from stress in the adoration of a cult leader, requires a considerable change in consciousness. And that is exactly what the cults offer—new consciousness, altered perceptions of reality, intense emotional states. Stay high forever! Tune in! Drop out! End all downers! The terminology is that of the hippie drug communalism of a few years back. The innocent utopianism of the flower children has all but disappeared. But very much with us are the search for the endless high, longer hairstyles, sexual permissiveness, casual and colorful dress, drug experimentation, playful curiosity about the occult. All have become acceptable cultural expressions for young and not-so-young Americans who have absolutely no intention of forsaking the mainstream. Lance Morrow has stated: "As always, the U.S. has demonstrated an infuriating . . . talent for absorbing and accommodating even those who began by wanting to tear the whole place down. Smoking marijuana is practically legal; the draft has been abolished." [4] Yesterday's incendiary radicals are running for public office, ranging from the U.S. Senate to the state treasury, from county assessor to city councilman.

Everyone has borrowed the language and style of the hippies. "*Get high*—daily existence is dull; so find the excitement of a 'peak experience.' *Tune in*—get in touch with your deepest feelings, with the world that surrounds you. *Drop out*—flaunt your distinctiveness against the forces that bind you to sterile conventions and rigid social roles. *End all downers*—change your way of living once and for all. Follow us and we will show you the true path to ecstatic self-fulfillment." So say psychodrama retreats, feminist groups, encounter sessions, assertiveness training, transcendental meditation, Primal Therapy, holistic health, Scientology, biofeedback, massage workshops, et cetera, ad infinitum. The list grows and grows.

Examine the use of this overworked language by two religious groups:

> We are love revolutionaries stoned on Jesus the liberator. We are no longer hung up on materialism. We have beat the system. We find Jesus neat, a gas, out of sight. We groove on God, experience his life-style, and find a permanent high. Jesus is the ultimate trip.
>
> *Stay high forever.* No more coming down. Practice Krishna Consciousness. Expand your consciousness by practicing the Transcendental Sound Vibration. Hare Krishna, Hare Krishna, . . . Hare Hare. . . . Try it and be blissful all the time. *Turn on* through music, dance, philosophy, science, religion, and prasadam (spiritual food). *Tune in.* Awaken your Transcendental Nature! . . . *Drop out* of movements employing artificially induced states of self-realization and expanded consciousness. . . . End all bringdowns, flip out and stay for eternity.[5]

The first quotation comes from the followers of the Jesus movement. The second is the message of Krishna Consciousness. To some observers, these statements represent sophisticated efforts on the part of new religious movements to translate their message into contemporary forms.[6] To me, they are advertising copy reminiscent of television commercials for pain relievers. They simply try too hard to catch the attention of their potential audience. But whether I like their propaganda or not, it is working.

The Cults Are on the Move

A young man selling candy and mounted butterflies came to my office. The solicitor's license that was pinned to his tie identified him as a representative of the Unification Church. I was on the phone when he arrived, and a member of the staff, knowing of my fascination with religious groups, asked him to have a seat until I was free. (The staffer later told me of how he fidgeted uncomfortably for the five minutes it took me to complete my call. After all, the sign on the door says Mental Health Association.)

I invited him into my office. After we exchanged introductions, I told him that I was "interested in the Unification Church" and asked him to tell me something about it. "What I can do," he responded, "is offer my personal testimony." He told me that he was from Ireland, that he had first "heard Principle" (the *Divine Principle* written by Sun Myung Moon) while he was studying civil engineering in Ireland. He had come to the United States to continue his studies but had abandoned engineering to devote himself full time to the work of the Unification Church.

Several times he attempted to explain basic church teaching to me—the nature of original sin, the divine plan for the restoration of the world to its intended perfection, the significance of the ministry and death of Jesus, the role of Sun Myung Moon. I tried to steer him away from the canned material that he had obviously memorized to get him to tell me what he is seeking, what his hopes and aspirations are as a Moonie. It was not hard to sense his intense idealism, his happiness, and his extreme wariness.

He told me that he wanted to help God achieve his purposes in the present age. "We don't believe in predestination," he explained. "God has given each of us unlimited free will. His plan for the world depends 95 percent upon himself and 5 percent on us. If we fail to contribute our 5 percent, his plan can be frustrated—as it was at the time of the sending of Jesus, who is truly his Son. After thousands of years of preparation through the preaching of the Old Testament prophets, when the promised Messiah finally came, he was rejected by his people."

This young man was wearing himself out as a fund-raiser for the Unification Church to see to it that God would not again be frustrated. As he left me sometime after five o'clock he told me, "I still have several hours of work ahead of me." He was disappointed that the rest of the offices in our building had closed for the day. While we talked, it had been clear to me that he had a genuine enthusiasm for what he was doing. He was selling candy and butterflies so that the Unification Church could flourish, so that it could become respectable. He was looking forward to the day when the church would have its own university in New York so that it could educate Unification Church doctors, lawyers, teachers, etc. "There are very few of us," he volunteered, "far fewer than you would think from what you read in the newspapers." Therefore, the current emphasis upon raising money and making converts is absolutely essential for the future. He predicted that someday the American church would be as multigenerational and prosperous as the Unification Church has become in Korea and Japan.

My young visitor was content with selling goods. For he was achieving humility, gaining self-discipline, and, above all, learning to love as Jesus had. "I have been rejected," he stated, "doors have been slammed in my face. I've been called names. But I remember what happened to the Son of God and how, when he was on the Cross, he prayed for those who had put him there."

When he spoke of his beliefs, of *Principle,* and Sun Myung Moon, he was relaxed, his face aglow with an infectious smile. When he attempted to answer my questions about concrete matters of the everyday life within the cult, he was hesitant. Every time I sensed that he was about to become devious, I would apologetically back off, telling him that I did not want to invade his privacy and that I knew that his church taught that a member should never tell an inquirer more than he was able to comprehend. "Yes," he said, "you see, we believe that a person is responsible for everything that he is told. If he hears the truth and is not prepared for it, he is nevertheless responsible to God. Besides, I know what you are going to ask, and I can't—." I interrupted, fully aware that he expected me to ask if Sun Myung Moon is the Lord of the Second Advent, the promised messiah of the last days. "No," I insisted, "you don't know what I am going to ask." And I led the discussion to other matters.

Attempts on my part to learn more of the doctrine and practices of the church made him uncomfortable. He did not seem interested in encouraging me to attend indoctrination sessions or in sending me literature. He did not want to turn me over to a "spiritual parent" who would seek to convert me. I guess that I am not the kind of young, unattached, malleable disciple they are seeking. The Moonies do not want people who are intellectually curious. They want zealous and idealistic recruits who will commit themselves today and learn more tomorrow. My visitor informed me that less stress is placed upon indoctrination of converts than was the case only months earlier. In what seemed an obvious contradiction of his disavowal of the concept of predestination, he declared: "If a person has good ancestors—saints and martyrs who have died for God—then he will be able to understand and live by *Principle*. If he has bad ancestors, then he will have a hard time. His understanding will be mostly intellectual, and his faith will be self-centered."

He had told me that he and a small group of Unification Church fund-raisers were living in the community in which I reside. Since I was leaving work for the day, I offered to drive him home. If I had thought for a moment, I would have known better. He expressed the fear that the Unification Church has of giving out addresses and phone numbers. "If people know where we are, they harass us, phone us at all hours, try to kidnap our members. We have to be careful," he related.

The last thing he expressed, before I offered to buy a box of peanuts and bid him farewell, was his fervent desire for a better world. "I want to marry someday, when the time is right," he said, "and raise children. But first, the world has to be straightened out so that it will be the right place for children to grow up. God bless you," and he was on his way.

There are thousands of Moonies and Hare Krishnas and Children of God and followers of other strange authoritarian cults. They ask everything of their followers: "Give up your family, your possessions, your career, your plans for the future. We will love you, feed you, clothe you, think for you, use your energies, and make you happy forever."

The cults are coming. They sound like the share-our-high-and-you-will-be-able-to-cope-with-anything sects of a few years ago. But they have gone beyond the self-centered quest for enlightenment of the consciousness-raisers and the preachers of personal salvation. The new cults are "total trips." Their key word is *self-abnegation* instead of *self-realization*. They demand obedience rather than belief or understanding. Get an individual to act like a member of the group for an hour, a day, a week, a month—and dogma, ritual, and religious experience will take care of themselves. The pathway to the abundant life in most sects begins with an intense religious experience, such as being "born again," and proceeds to an explanation of that experience in terms of the doctrines of the group, followed by the day-to-day routine of living in accordance with group customs. The new cults examined in these pages have reversed the usual process. What they are proclaiming is: "Live our daily life until you are ready to learn what we believe. In time, you shall know the truth, and you shall be saved." This is the essential message of the cults.

II. THE UNIFICATION CHURCH OF SUN MYUNG MOON

The Great Escape

The phone rang early one Saturday morning, shocking me into consciousness. I groped for the receiver. "Hello," I croaked with annoyance. "Lowell, it's Mike. I'm on the run. I've just escaped. I'm at a drive-in market about a hundred miles from your house. Can I come over? I've got to talk to someone. Maybe I'm making a terrible mistake running away. Can I come over?"

Mike is my oldest friend. Even though he is a decade younger than I, we have always been able to share our deepest feelings. It has been years since we both lived in the same city. So we make it a practice to get together around the first of each year. If our paths cross during the year, fine. If not, we always know that we can depend on our

Poster promoting Unification Church rally.

annual get-togethers. We have lent each other money, provided lodging for each other as each of us has traveled about the country, offered each other advice during times of personal crisis, comforted each other in the wake of family tragedies.

Mike will be thirty in a year. He has been married and divorced twice. A few years back, he gave up a promising career in banking to become an artist. His oil paintings are priced at about two hundred dollars apiece. Some months he sells one or two. Some months he doesn't sell any. When he runs out of cash, he often works for a temporary employment agency that finds him office jobs with various businesses. He does not like to feel committed or tied down, or so he tells me. He prizes "being my own boss; doing what I want to do when I want to do it." He gets terribly lonely at times, and loneliness makes him vulnerable.

I had never heard such urgency in his voice. He sounded frightened and confused. "Get over here as soon as you can," I told him. A few hours later he arived in his old beaten-up automobile, which was overflowing with his earthly goods—clothes, cooking utensils, books, paints, brushes. I almost failed to recognize the figure that stepped from that derelict car. His usual beard and long hair were gone. The tortoiseshell-framed glasses that he had worn in one form or another for fifteen years had been replaced with old-fashioned rimless glasses. Something about him frightened and confused me upon first impression.

My wife and the boys were shopping when Mike arrived. So we had a chance to talk without interruption. And talk he did—for six hours, which was long after their return.

"I had to get away," he started. "I was at this farm in Boonville. They lock the gate. But when they had it open for a bus, I just made a run for it. Maybe I'm doing a terrible thing. Maybe the devil is tempting me."

The devil? Why would Mike, whose background was liberal Jewish and whose own personal quest had led him in the direction of Primal Therapy and Eastern spirituality, be worried about the devil? Little by little he gained his composure, and his story unfolded. He began: "Last July I was living in Berkeley, and I was disconnecting from a job I had as a clerk. I was finding out that wasn't who I am. That's a keynote to my hooking up with anything—and especially these people, the Moonies. I've continually been searching for who I am and how I fit in.

"I was spending a lot of time that summer drinking. And I was finding that it was the only way that I could settle down at the end of a day, the only way I could face—or not face—what I was having to deal with. And what I was having to deal with then was feeling lost and not belonging to anything. I have this real strong desire to belong, to be part of something. I've always been that way. I guess I'm still looking for that."

The Elephant Bus

One evening Mike walked down to Telegraph Avenue where he spotted a colorfully decorated bus emblazoned with the name "The Elephant Bus." He walked over. Inside were twenty happy-looking young people. "The bus looked nice inside. It was well decorated, homey. And everybody was singing. Everyone on that bus was real clean-cut looking. All the men were wearing slacks and sport shirts. Those who wore glasses had rimless ones—like the pair I'm wearing. The men had short haircuts. And the women were dressed well in skirts and blouses. Clean-cut all-American types."

Mike was handed a small book titled *The Elephant Book*, which retold the well-known Asian fable of the blind men and the elephant. The message was simple: Everyone has a partial understanding of the truth. Not until an individual knows the whole picture is it possible for him to orient his life. We are all looking for the truth so that we can establish a better world. Mike visited with them for about half an hour. The only information he could get about the group or its purpose was that they lived in "an alternative community." They told him that they had a house in San Francisco where anyone who was interested was invited to come for dinner. "We're trying to make a new world," they cryptically explained. "We're building communities throughout the country, and we're interested in people who are willing to make a commitment to our ideas." No further elaboration was offered.

Weeks later, Mike quit his job. "I was up in the air, didn't know what to do," he related. So, finding the address of the group on *The Elephant Book,* he decided to pay them a visit. The location was an elegant Victorian mansion in San Francisco. He was greeted by a young woman who asked many questions about his reason for visiting. She gave him some general information about the group, their exploration of "alternative life-styles, more meaningful relationships, deeper communication in marriage and family life." It sounded good to Mike. "There was no mention of anything religious or in any way connected with any group. So I felt no reason for being on guard." Mike related. "And I was looking for alternatives to the failing life-style I was leading. I was not making it at something I didn't believe in—being a clerk. And I also was not making it at something I did believe in—being an artist. I was looking for something to believe in, for brothers and sisters, for a family where I could fit and belong. And that's what they were offering."

He spent an hour talking about "the family" that lived in the house, some of whom worked in family-owned business enterprises; others spending their days recruiting new members for the community. "I was interested," Mike recalled, "by everything I heard and saw. They were so *orderly* looking. The house looked nice. It looked so *middle-class*." He stayed for dinner. There were 150 people in the house. "There was a high energy level. Everyone was sharing their experiences. They were so enthusiastic. They all looked nice and respectable and clean. Gosh, it felt good. I was asked to help in the kitchen. Everybody was so into what they were doing—doing it because they wanted to. I could tell.

"I knew that I was being checked out. Three different people engaged me in conversation, one after another. As they walked away, they went over to one of the older people and reported on what I had said. I could tell that I was being *chosen*, because of my intelligence and ability to communicate; I was being *picked*." Then Muffin, an attractive young woman, joined him. He would later discover that she had been assigned to him as his "spiritual parent." He recounted, "She was put there to hold my hand, to guide me, to answer any questions, to put down any anxieties I had, to lead me to their way."

After dinner a woman spoke on making the world a better place for our children. Another speaker gave "the elephant speech"—basically the same message as *The Elephant Book*. Afterward the guests were told about a farm commune owned by the group in a nearby county. "It is called Ideal City," Mike stated. "What a great name—Ideal City. Everyone is looking for their ideal city, their ideal relationships, their ideal family. That's what they were selling. I was asked if I wanted to take a bus that very night and spend some time up there. 'Sure, why not?' I said. I had no place else to go, nothing else to do, no commitments, no responsibilities. I figured, Why not?"

Ideal City

Two hours later Mike and seven other young people were on their way to Ideal City, which is located near Boonville. "Everyone was happy. We were all singing." Mike only half noticed the locked gate and guardhouse at the entrance. Inside was a huge farm commune. Men and women were immediately separated: the men sent to sleep at a large converted chicken coop; the women to a fifteen-by-forty-foot modular building. "My first impression was, 'How super!' Everything was so spick-and-span, so clean—righteously clean! Here were thousands of acres with paths leading into the hills, swinging bridges over creeks, evidence of a lot of careful labor."

Outdoor lunch and lecture at the Boonville training center north of San Francisco.

At six the next morning, everyone was awakened and taken by truck to a large, high-raftered barn. "And here's where the indoctrination starts; here's where the *brain-*

washing starts," said Mike. What followed was a three-day seminar consisting of lectures to the entire group, followed by small group discussions of each lecture in which ten to fifteen people were guided by a leader and an assistant leader. The leader and the assistant questioned each visitor to find out how he or she was responding, to involve each visitor. "The lectures started out with where the world's at, why the world's here right now, and what our responsibility is. We have the responsibility to create the perfect world, and the way we have to create it is by forming the perfect family, entering into a perfect marital relationship, and becoming perfect mothers and fathers and creating the perfect children. And the creation of the perfect children will then allow the next generation to create the perfect family. If we can create the family, then we can create the perfect city, the perfect state, the perfect nation, the perfect world; everything will be perfect if only we will follow these ways of being. We were told that we are so steeped in sin that the only hope for the world lies with our children. We are lost, but we are chosen by God to come to Ideal City. Now, for the first time, God starts to sneak into all this. And God wants us because we want to make God happy. That's important: for us to be happy makes God happy, and we realize that we are making him happy which makes us even happier, and that makes God even happier and on and on."

The fervor and excitement increased from lecture to lecture. "By the third day of the lectures—believe it or not—80 to 90 percent of the people there are sold, jumping up and down, yelling and cheering. Everything is presented in such a way that it produces *enthusiasm*. I remember one lecture on the third day about how when we really get it together we will be able to make America a beautiful, wonderful place. And by the end of the lecture everyone was standing there filled with emotion: some people with tears in their eyes, singing 'God Bless America.' And how wonderful it felt!"

Each lecture session begins with appropriate songs to set the mood. Each session ends with a couple of songs that reinforce the mood. Mike proceeded: "One of the lectures on the second day is about why this old world is so messed up. They were saying that everything is where it's at right now because we're sinners. We're all sinners because we're concerned with ourselves and not concerned with pleasing God. And this is why we're lost and why the world is so messed up. And that lecture I remember because it caused more people to freak out, to be really upset than any other lecture. That was the zinger! It's either face up to who you are or forget this whole thing. Admit how rotten and misguided you have been. Accept what we have to say or be damned. For if you leave us right now, God will really be angry because he has chosen you. And if you have any thoughts contrary to what we are telling you or have any doubts, then you had better watch out, for those thoughts are not coming from you but from the devil. I had never heard anything like that before. It was really scary."

While Mike attended the lectures, his spiritual parent was with him constantly. He later found out that between sessions she was reporting his reactions to her supervisors. After the third and final day of lectures, Mike was invited to stay on. "I wanted to stay. I felt that this was really great. I was excited. I felt wanted, appreciated. I was one of the bright, shining stars among the new people there. I was cared about. People were showing a lot of attention to me as a person, listening to my ideas, praising me." He explained to the leaders that first he had to go back to

Berkeley to take care of some personal matters: pay his rent, get his belongings, say good-bye to friends. Muffin was sent with him to ensure his return to Ideal City. He resisted, arguing that there was no need to send her along but was told that if he wanted to be one of them, that was the way it would have to be. He desired to be with them; so he complied.

Mike's belongings were taken from him at the guardhouse so that they could be checked for contraband, e.g., incendiaries, firearms, tobacco, alcohol, literature opposed to the teachings of the group. Mike was bothered, but again he complied. He explained, "I accepted because I was being accepted."

The next morning Mike discovered that there were four hundred new recruits and two hundred established members present. "We were all called out to this giant field at 5:30 in the morning. Our names were called as everyone cheered." The same lecture series followed but at an accelerated pace—three days of material presented in two days. On the second day, there was a game of dodge ball, which is the only sport allowed. At the end of this second exposure to the lectures, "it got down to the nitty-gritty: Are you staying or are you going? Each affirmative decision set off an explosion of celebration. Everyone gleefully join arms, sing songs, jump up and down."

Each day followed an established pattern. Reveille was at six. "You jumped out of your sleeping bag, and you screamed at the top of your lungs, 'Good morning, God. Praise the Lord!' Everybody but everybody did this." An open-air assembly followed with more cheering and the singing of "Oh, What a Beautiful Morning!" "Zip-a-dee-doo-dah," or "The Sound of Music." Then it was time for morning exercises. " 'Hey, you over there,' a voice would ring out, 'you're not giving one-oh-oh' (100 percent). 'Don't forget that yesterday's 100 percent is today's 90 percent. You've got to give more. Be more alive.'" Breakfast was served. The day was consumed with lectures, group meetings, lunch, more lectures, more group meetings, two hours or more of manual labor followed by early-evening lectures until dinner, then ecstatic singing and praise like a Pentecostal tent revival. And, finally, time for bed.

The routine was unvaried from day to day—except for Fridays. "Every Friday night was a surprise party for God," Mike explained. "Money was collected from those who had it. 'You have fifty dollars. Far out. We can buy fifty dollars worth of ice cream for God's surprise party. That will really make God happy.' Everything was being done for God, and if you had anything to contribute, you gave it for God, to make him happy. The surprise parties were fun. Everybody got to get up to entertain. Noah, who ran things there, would call on us one by one. He was like Grandpa, a really strong figure. And everyone treated him with respect. But I could never get into that. I felt a real conflict."

The material presented at the week-long lecture series was identical to what had previously been given, except that now the Bible was introduced to buttress each of the teachings. "Look at how the present world condition was prophesied. The Lord of the Second Advent is coming." Moments of exultation began to alternate with periods of grief and lamentation as the theme of the rejection of Jesus was developed. "'He was the Messiah, the avatar,' we were told, 'but he was rejected, and the same thing is happening right now.' It was clear to me that they were saying that the Lord of the Second Advent is already here. 'Who is he?' I wondered. When I asked the leaders, I was told, 'We'll let you know.' 'Wow,' I thought, 'they're going to tell me; I'm going to find out who the Lord of the Second Advent is!' "

Confrontation

Mike's joy was tempered by an unsought confrontation with the group leaders. In a moment of happiness, he had hugged one of the women. Three leaders rushed over and harshly parted the couple. "We don't do that here," they insisted. "This is God's land, and God doesn't want us to do that here." Mike was humiliated and deeply upset. "I resented being treated like a child," he commented. But allowing oneself to act like a child had its compensations in group approval and acceptance. Still the resentment clung to Mike. He explained the action of the leaders further: "You see, we were being taught that we weren't perfect enough to form relationships with one another. And that when we got to be perfect then we had to form a perfect relationship, a perfect marriage. Until that time, there could be no desires. They were only tools of the devil."

Mike was assigned a new spiritual parent, *one of the same sex*. Because he was asking so many questions he was given a hard-core, longtime follower. "Amazingly, they found someone in their group that acted, felt, and looked like me. People thought that we were brothers. But after two weeks, I blew him away." Mike expressed so many doubts, raised so many questions, that his full-time guide suffered his own identity crisis!

Group pressure maintained conformity, ensured that rules were kept, set limits to behavior. It was not necessary to utter the guidelines aloud. The acceptance or rejection of several hundred people, all agreed on the same set of ideas, is a powerfully coercive force. As much as he resented being told what to do and when to do it, Mike stifled his hostile feelings for the sake of the supportive feelings. Only after three weeks at the commune was he permitted to leave the grounds as part of a small group (six recruits and six spiritual parents) sent to witness to an elderly couple in a nearby town. In the few hours he was away from the commune, Mike had a strong sense of yearning for the minor, accustomed pleasures of his existence prior to his days at Ideal City: ice-cream cones, time to sit down and watch a baseball game, casual conversations with friends. "I didn't express any of this," he said. "I just went back to the same old routine. And the routine felt good. It kept me busy, filled my days. And there was always somebody for me to talk with, somebody to be with.

"I noticed that every Saturday night those people who had been at the commune for three or four weeks were invited to a *special* lecture. 'What's happening?' I would ask them. 'Oh, you're not ready for it yet. You don't need to know,' one of the leaders would tell me." If Mike's questions persisted, a leader would be dispatched to Noah in order to seek further instructions for dealing with Mike.

Before Mike was invited to the special lecture, an incident occurred that totally disrupted the group. Mike had a psychic experience. It should be noted that he has always believed in extraordinary occurrences such as precognition, telekinesis, and telepathy. Mike stated: "I can't explain how it happened, but one Friday night I was asleep, and suddenly I was having the most intense dream that I have ever known. No. It wasn't a dream. It was an 'out of the body' experience. I rose up, looked at myself lying on the floor there in this chicken coop. And before me was a house—there in the air. It was absolutely real, not like watching a movie. I walked to the house. I opened up the door. And in the house was Sun Myung Moon drinking tea! Now let me make one thing clear, I had never heard of Sun Myung Moon during my stay at Ideal City. His name had never been mentioned. But here was Sun Myung Moon, and he asked me to come in and talk to him and have a cup of tea. I said, 'Who are you?' And he said, 'I am Rev. Sun Myung Moon.' Then he told me that I was ready to know what was going on there. And the next thing I knew it ended. I was in the air, and I was going back into my body. I reached out, touched the floor, realized that this had all truly, truly happened. Then I was lying back in bed, and I couldn't understand it. But I accepted it completely."

The next day Mike went to one of the leaders and recounted his "revelatory" experience. The leader was amazed but concerned as to the source of the information Mike had obtained. "Well, it caused a furor," Mike recalled. "I was called aside, and for one day I was questioned and grilled and checked out. It was a really intense day of upper-level people—people who were brought in from San Francisco to find out who I was and what I was doing there. They were afraid of my causing a problem. And I had mentioned to somebody else, another newcomer, my dream and that Sun Myung Moon was behind the whole show. And word got out. It really tore things up. And the leaders really got mad. And people who were finding this out were remembering all the negative stuff that they had heard about Sun Myung Moon and the Moonies. They began planning to leave. So I was a troublemaker. I didn't mean to be. It just came out that way."

The "Secret" Revealed

The next Saturday night found Mike at the secret lecture for the chosen. "This was the most intense, the most emotionally appealing lecture I have ever witnessed. Noah tells us the life story of Sun Myung Moon." So now for the first time the "secret" was out in the open. "We were told about his trials and tribulations and his Jesus-like character and his spiritual phenomena and how he truly is the Lord of the Second Advent, how he has been chosen by God. We were told that the doctrines we had learned were Sun Myung Moon's and that he has given us all this so that we can help him create this new world for God. And everyone was sold. They were cheering for Sun Myung Moon. But I said, 'Nonsense! I don't believe it. I just can't.' "

The graduates of the secret session were instructed to keep the new information to themselves. They were then sent to the city for further indoctrination and for assignments as missionaries. Soon they would be spiritual parents and bring their flock back to Ideal City to start the cycle anew. But there was no such assignment for Mike. He was sent back to square one, to start the basic indoctrination again. He was getting bored and resentful, and he let the leaders know it. He wanted to progress to whatever the next rung of the ladder might me. "I'm tired of this. I know every lecture by heart. What are you going to do with me? I want to go back to painting. I want to do my thing," he protested. He was told, "But you have to give up *your* thing and do what *God* wants you to do." "Well, God must want me to paint," Mike insisted. "So a compromise was worked out. They were going to send me to another city to start an art-supply store, to teach painting, and to paint for them. And that was going to be my use—unless wanted to go to upstate New York and study to become a minister. Well, this was kicked around for a couple of days, and when the list of assignments came out, I found out that I was still going to spend another week there. And I made the decision—impulsively. And on Saturday morning while everyone was cheering and yelling and welcoming the people who had come in for the weekend lectures, I gathered up my sleeping bag, got my car, found where they were keeping my belongings, put them in the car, and drove to the gate—only to find out that it was locked! That did it! I knew that I had to get out of there, that this was enough for me. I was done with being told how to live and with not being allowed to think for myself. I was angry—angry that I was being treated like a child. So I hid my car behind a building and waited for the next time the gate was opened. A bus came in pulling a trailer; both of them were filled with people. And as soon as the bus and the trailer cleared the gate, I threw the car into gear, floored the accelerator, and was gone. It was like *The Great Escape*. And I heard sirens going off!"

Mike concluded, "The first thing I did was go to a drive-in place and have two cups of coffee, cigarettes, and a bottle of beer. I got a newspaper and some ice cream. Then I called you."

A Psychiatrist Among the Moonies

Confirmation of Mike's experience came from another source a few months later. Samuel J. Klein, M.D., is staff psychiatrist and chief of adolescent services for a large suburban county. He is respected for his work with "incorrigible young people." Dr. Klein is an intelligent, open, and kind man. A year ago, if you had asked him what he thought about attempts to deprogram converts to religious cults, he would have told you that he respected the right of each person to make his own choice. An individual who joins the Moonies or the Hare Krishnas or the Children of God is exercising his or her own free will, and no one should interfere with that freedom. If you had argued that the cults were brainwashing their converts, he would have insisted that the follower of a cult is free to leave at any time and that it would be an invasion of the individual's human dignity and autonomy to attempt to compel the convert to forsake his or her newfound way of life.

Dr. Klein has changed his mind. In his spare time, he is speaking before parents' groups at churches and synagogues, warning the public against the practices of the Unification Church of Sun Myung Moon. "After what I have seen for myself," he declares, "I believe that the Unification Chuch is effectively using coercive persuasion, thought control, hypnosis, induced phobias." Such brainwashing techniques, he asserts, have been fully developed by the Moonies; and they work. "People have a right to choose," he adds, "but I don't think the Moonies are exercising choice. I think that Ted Patrick and the deprogrammers go too far. But I understand what they are trying to do: Fight fire with fire. I now favor giving the Moonies a chance to hear other opinions, have contact with their families, and be exposed to opposite points of view." And having witnessed courtroom dramas of parents seeking to be appointed conservator so that they could remove their children from the clutches of the Unification Church, he feels strongly that Moonies are held by the sect under powerful mind control. Their methods, he asserts, are reminiscent of the techniques used against American prisoners during the Korean War and in China today by the Communist regime as an ongoing process of maintaining total conformity to the official policy in thought, word, and deed.

Dr. Klein has learned about the Moonies from concerned parents of converts, by speaking with numerous former Moonies, by observing members of the Unification Church at conservatorship hearings in the San Francisco courts. And he has also experienced the Unification Church from within. After the movement was called to his attention by the frantic mother of a convert, Dr. Klein attended indoctrination sessions at the group's retreat center in Boonville, California. "For a year I was being manipulated," he says. "I was love-bombed." For this is the way of the Moonies, to attract with the gift of "total approval and affection."

According to Klein, potential converts are approached on the streets by clean-cut, wholesome young people who are selling flowers, peanuts, or literature. The money is being raised, they claim, for "youth education," "libraries," or "drug-abuse programs." And who can be against education, books, or anything that will divert people from drugs? An appeal is thus made to the individual's sense of idealism. Further, the well-groomed salesperson offers what Klein terms "a visual parental model." For example, the men wear white shirts and ties. Their hair is short and carefully combed. "They're something right out of the fifties," Klein states. Finally, the lure of the opposite sex is offered. An attractive female Moonie engages a man in conversation. A personable young man moves nearer to an interested woman.

Soon the potential convert is invited to dinner at a nearby apartment or to spend a weekend in the country in order to share "an ideal family experience." No mention is made of the Unification Church, Klein notes. For instance, the literature distributed in Boonville is published by the Re-education Center. Reports Klein: "At a dinner or weekend retreat, the individual is offered all the attention, affection, and approval that anyone could ever have craved. He or she is encouraged to have a good time, 'Take off your shoes; be silly.' The atmosphere is like a well-run summer camp. You sing a lot of camp songs, act childlike, simple; have your decisions made for you. 'Get into the experience,' the group advises. 'Don't be negative. Turn off your head, just feel it, feel it, feel it.' " Hymns are sung with a Pentecostal fervor accompanied by a heavily amplified rock beat. The visitor is subjected to a "nonstop, forty-eight-hour marathon indoctrination." The teachings of the group are set forth with a ferocious intensity and rhythmic force like a hammer pounding away at an anvil. Questions are parried deftly: "Gee, that's a great question. It really shows that you're paying attention. It will be answered in the next session." A few basic doctrines are repeated and repeated until the audience practically recites them in unison, until the newcomer unconsciously anticipates the conclusion of the speaker's thought in mid sentence.

There is little time for sleep and no time for reflection, Klein recalls. No one is permitted to be alone. Contact with the outside world is not allowed. The author attempted to phone a friend who was attending a session to wish him a happy birthday. I received excuses and evasion and, finally, the promise that my phone call would be returned. My friend was never told that I had called. Remorselessly the entire group plows on and on. For the newcomers, claims Klein, "are being imprinted."

What and How the Moonies Teach

The teachings of the Moonies are fascinating—a blend of Christian theology, Korean folk religion, confused speculations, social activism, and heretical innovations. They can readily be summarized in twenty to thirty pages as Frederick Sontag has done in his appreciative study of the cult.[1] The problem that I have is more with *how* the Moonies teach than with *what* they teach. Using a concept of progressive revelation, the hearer is told no more than he can absorb given his level of consciousness. Great stress is placed upon the necessity of preparation for each level of instruction. Hence, the doctrines of the Unification Church are presented with a frustrating lack of openness and at a pace that insults the intelligence of all but the dimmest mind. First, the lectures are given in the least offensive form—with little reference to God or religion. Next God, Jesus, and the Bible creep in. Then religious concepts are heavily stressed. Finally, after weeks, the name of Sun Myung Moon is introduced.

There is no question that the Moonies are deceptive in their indoctrination as well as in their fund-raising. They can rationalize their reticence to sail under their true colors in a number of ways. The Unification Church and Mr. Moon have received so much negative publicity that visitors and donors would be frightened away; Satan could harness an audience's prejudices as a basis for persecuting the Moonies; Jesus counseled *his* disciples against casting pearls before swine. But, the fact remains that Moonies are evasive, less than totally honest, and prone to an ethnic of "the ends justifying the means." Whatever their motivations, the Moonies have won themselves more suspicion and hostility because of their untruthfulness than for any other reason. It is about time that the word of Sun Myung Moon filtered down to his followers on the local level. As Moon proclaimed in an interview with Dr. Sontag:

> Honesty comes first. . . .
> A member must say that he is a member of the Unification Church and that he is the follower of Sun Myung Moon. If he doesn't have the courage to say it, he is not worthy of me. . . . I can understand why such things may have happened in the face of persecution, but I do not condone such action.[2]

What does the Unification Church teach? Who is Sun Myung Moon? What role does he play? Briefly we may summarize the major tenets as follows. God is described by Moon in explicitly anthropomorphic terms. God suffers, weeps, feels frustration, knows joy and happiness, even laughs. His will can be thwarted. He created man in his image to be one with him in feeling, thought, and action. It was his original intention that Adam and Eve would be united with his blessing and give birth to sinless children, thereby establishing a sinless family and a sinless world. The human race was to live in perfect harmony with God, with one another, and with the Creation.

But none of this came to pass because of the Fall. Tempted by the archangel Lucifer, Adam and Eve entered into illicit love, coming together as husband and wife without the blessing of God. Hence, their children and all their descendants are not the children of God but the children of Satan. Satan, not God, is the lord of this world. God attempts to restore mankind to himself by sending the Messiah. But before the Messiah may come, mankind must pay indemnity for sin so that the conditions are proper for the restoration of the Creation. History records the repeated failure on the part of man to make reparations.

Hence, restoration has been postponed again and again.

Jesus of Nazareth came as the Second Adam, the only Son of God. Through him, God sought to restore the Creation to himself, to begin the perfect family whose sinless offspring would reunite spiritual and material reality to himself. But the mission of Jesus was a failure. He attracted the wrong social classes to himself, won the hostility of the political and religious leaders of the people, and failed to win even the complete support of John the Baptist. The Crucifixion is a sign of his failure. Yet through his crucifixion and his resurrection, Jesus did accomplish the salvation of mankind's spiritual being (but not of the material world in which we live). Another cycle has come round. The time is right for the appearance of the Lord of the Second Advent. We are living in the last days. A new age has dawned. We can communicate with God once more. God is depending upon us to contribute our part to the restoration of creation. If we fail, his purpose will once again be frustrated, his heart once again be broken as it was by the rejection and crucifixion of Jesus.

The central figure in the redemptive acts that are occurring before our very eyes will be born of a chosen people, the nation of Korea. The Lord of the Second Advent will lead us to salvation not only of the spiritual world but of every aspect of existence including politics, commerce, the arts, science, etc. He will marry and produce sinless children. He and his followers will create a perfect family, a perfect nation, a perfect world. Godless communism and illicit sexuality—the two chief obstacles to the rule of God—will be vanquished. And all this is in process of happening now!

Look carefully—but not too carefully—at the ingredients of the Unification Church plan for the restoration of the creation of mankind. Contemporary man is being offered a vision of a better world, a way to return to an ideal state of human nature, a leader to show us the way, a concrete plan for getting there, a strategy for recruiting disciplined followers—in sum, the dawning of a new era. But before any of the details has been revealed, the prospective disciple is invited to commit himself totally, to join the Unified Family, to become a part of the elite band. All will be revealed in time. Don't think. Just sing along:

> Gonna build a kingdom on this sad old ground;
> Gonna build a kingdom all around!
> Gonna call it heaven 'cause that's what it'll be,
> A place of beauty, peace and joy for you and me.[3]

As we have seen, weeks pass before the new family members realize that they have joined the Unification Church, that the leader is Sun Myung Moon, that the concrete plan is Moon's 536-page revelation *Divine Principle*. Many more weeks follow of study sessions, thought-control groups at which family members openly share their secrets and fund-raising and convert-seeking excursions into the streets of the city. Little by little, the "truth" is proclaimed. Jesus of Nazareth failed. He will not return. It is up to the Lord of the Second Advent to usher in the Kingdom. The world need no longer wait for him. He is here already. He was born in Korea not long ago. Not even *Divine Principle* discloses his identity. Can you figure out who he is? Do you share in the unproclaimed secret of his identity? (The only *overt* claim made in Moonie literature is that Sun Myung Moon is "God's messenger.")

The Perfect Family

"Jesus was a failure," preaches a movement that claims to be "based on Christian beliefs and ideology." The

Crucifixion should never have occurred. Jesus allied himself with the wrong kind of people. His plans were incomplete and impractical. A dead Savior cannot restore mankind to its ideal nature. Hence, salvation depends on the Lord of the Second Advent. His followers will be the cream of the cream. His movement will win the support of social, political, and economic leaders. There will be trials and tribulations for a time, but in the end a crown without a cross awaits the Father and his Unified Family.

And who are the American recruits to the elite family of Father Moon? They are young, in their early and mid twenties. For the most part, they are college educated. Few are black or Spanish-surnamed. Few are street people or derelicts. Moon's elite is not made up of burnt-out dopers. About a third are Jewish; another third Roman Catholic. They are lonely, college-aged men and women, some living away from home for the first time in their lives. Many are recovering from a recent personal crisis such as a breakup with a boyfriend or girl friend, an academic or job-related setback, perhaps a recent divorce. They are anxious, stress ridden, overcome by adulthood and its responsibilities. The message is clear: Let the Family be your mother, father, sister, and brother. Let the Family direct your energies, plan your day, plot your future, select your mate, and make a better person of you. For the Unification Church is determined not only to build the Kingdom but to reconstruct the being of its every member. Welcome, pilgrim, to the ordeal of change. By joining the perfect Family of Father Moon, you have chosen sides. You and all who follow the Unified Family belong to God. The world belongs to Satan. Thus it has been since the beginning.

Jesus came as the Messiah in an attempt to restore mankind to the divine plan for a perfect family. But he failed and died without offspring. The Lord of the Second Advent will rectify Christ's mistake. He will establish the perfect family. He and his wife—Moon is married and has several children—will provide an example for all others to follow. Marriage is not only a divinely blessed union of man and woman, it is central to the salvation of mankind as Moon perceives it.

All marriages within the Unification Church are arranged by the church and must be approved by Mr. Moon. But before an individual is allowed to marry, he or she must produce at least three spiritual children, that is, three converts to the Unified Family. In this manner—as well as through the later production of physical children—a disciple of Moon's obeys the biblical injunction "to be fruitful and multiply." However, even obedience to the teaching of the Unification Church does not truly sanctify marriage. For according to Moon no marriage in the present satanic world is recognized by God. It would be desirable for husband and wife to each go a separate way, proclaiming the message of Moon. In what must be described as a hopelessly confused and confusing doctrine, Moon sets forth the view that it would be best if husband and wife refrained from intercourse for seven *years* but that they be permitted to "receive [this] blessing" after only seven *months*. Moon admits that he liberalized this standard only after he himself married. In any event, there is strong encouragement to produce offspring.

The War Between God and Satan

The world in which the Moonie lives is one where opposed spiritual forces vie for supremacy. All that furthers the building of the perfect family is of God; all that interferes is of Satan. There is a constant war being waged throughout the world (e.g., materialistic communism versus the more spiritually sympathetic democracies). The same war goes on within the world (e.g., materialistic communism versus the more spiritually sympathetic democracies). The same war goes on within the soul of each human being, including the members of the Unification Church. This ceaseless struggle must be taken in utmost seriousness. Communism must be crushed, and every political structure that sets itself against communism must be supported. Hence, Moon's strong support of the present South Korean regime. (It should be noted that Moon was a prisoner of the North Korean government during the Korean conflict.)

Likewise, the individual must guard his soul against every infiltration by satanic forces. New converts are totally separated from the world of Satan: television, telephones, newspapers, and, above all, their parents. They are taught to suppress all doubts. They are encouraged to surrender time, money, energy, life itself to the Unified Family. *Not giving enough is the cardinal sin.* Difficult goals are set for each member. So many souls are to be won by such a date. So many dollars are to be raised by soliciting contributions or selling flowers, floral arrangements, candles, or other products of church-controlled industries.

Nothing is more devastating to a Moonie than the words "You are not giving enough. You are selfish, insincere, evil." Group pressure can be enormous. The thoughts that the disciple has shared with the group can be turned against him. Indemnity must be paid for every shortcoming. According to Moon, God never forgives man unconditionally for his sins. One must pay. The principle is God's, but the payment is exacted by Satan. States Moon:

> The Law of Indemnity is like bankruptcy. Imagine that you owe someone $1,000, but all you can scrape together is $50. Your creditor accepts what you have and forgives the balance. This is what God does. Satan, however, is not as generous as God. He will not forgive anything. He demands 100 percent payment, and, if it is not paid willingly, he will exact it in the form of illness, pain, worry, fear, doubt, inconveniences, moods, depression, and many other diverse and subtle methods. There is, however, a way in which these debts can be paid off quickly. Conscious payment of physical indemnity of restitution in everything we do removes Satan's opportunity to attack us. God will not let Satan claim more than his due.[4]

Such divinely decreed fines can be levied in the form of extra household chores or days of fasting. But let the slightest worry or pain invade the mind of the disciple, and the sense of unpaid indemnity will multiply. Thus, a religious experience that begins as regression to a blissful state of childlike innocence is step by step transformed into a compulsive, dread-filled struggle to regain contantly a sense of security and acceptance. Under the pressure of the group and of stresses that build up within, a compulsive pattern of behavior emerges. Such internal and external controls crush autonomy, leaving the disciple totally dependent upon the Unified Family.

Self-sacrifice offers refuge from the demands of the "real world." Ask the Moonie recruits what they have found and they will tell you, "This is the first truly satisfying thing I have ever done." Mike explains: "I can understand how they feel—in our culture where everything is artificial and the stimulations are commercial. The Moonies offer a chance to give up what was before, to receive group acceptance, to find order and structure, to add emotional intensity to one's life." But for Mike the Moonie answer does not work. He muses, "I think that the real world is harsher, demands more, presents more problems, offers more choices than the world of the Moonies."

Self-sacrifice on the part of recruits has also established the Unification Church as the most financially secure of the new cults. Moon has created a worldwide financial conglomerate based upon the donated services of his followers. The financial empire of the Unification Church is far flung across our country with real estate, fishing fleets, construction businesses, the largest office-cleaning firm in one major city, landscaping services, candle manufacturing, flower and candy sales. As Mike observes, "One of the reasons the Moonies are successful is that every member is made to see the value of hard work—'yesterday's 100 percent is today's 90 percent.' " Each member is assigned an income-producing job, that is, a job that will produce income for the Unification Church.

Most of the Moonies come from middle-class backgrounds where the work ethic was instilled in them. The majority are college graduates with degrees in everything from engineering to the fine arts. Many have advanced professional training in medicine, law, theology, etc. Mike noticed: "They found out that once they had their degrees, their idealism could not be put to immediate use. It was a hindrance. So they put that idealism to full use with the Moonies." But it is unlikely that there will be any greater match of interests and talents among the Moonies than there is in the free-enterprise marketplace. Whatever work one is assigned, they are encouaged by the group to do it joyfully. "Do it for God and make him happy," they are taught. And give it everything that you have. For the redemption of the world is 95 percent God's responsibility and 5 percent man's. Man's failure is enough to disrupt the entire divine plan. Hence, the burden upon each individual is enormous. There is no slacking off, no rest breaks, no excuses. God is counting on the Moonie to build the perfect family, city, nation, and world. At least one critic has described the Moon version of the work ethic as "a pretty good device to get people to dig ditches, cut down trees, work in the kitchen, labor in church-owned businesses, or sell merchandise in the streets. What a rationale for getting people to earn money and give it to the group. 'We're doing it for God.' What an interesting way to get yourself a group of slaves!"

An outgrowth of the constant demand for total effort is intense self-loathing. The bucolic serenity of Ideal City or any Moonie community is constantly punctuated by the frenzied weeping and wailing of distraught disciples who beat their breasts and call out to God to forgive them for not giving enough. The standard is nothing less than perfection. Each follower is to be like Jesus, a perfect Son of God.

Are the Moonies Brainwashed?

Observations by outsiders of such compulsive dedication had led them to the charge that the Moonies are *brainwashed*. The reader will recall that Mike used the very word in speaking of his experience. Samuel Klein has come to the conclusion that the Moonies are systematically stripped of their free will, subjected to thought-control techniques, induced into states of hypnosis by the indoctrination sessions. The author asked Mike if he agreed with Klein's verdict. Mike wrote to me:

> I hesitate to say it is true. We in our society are brainwashed about nearly everything. We can't watch television or read a magazine or go to a movie or even walk down a street

without seeing something that tells us how we should act and what we should have. Within the Moonies there is a great deal of order. If one lives with any group for a while, one soon finds out what acceptable behavior is, what the key phrases are, how to communicate. The Moonies are no more guilty of brainwashing than is a sixth-grade class in a public school. Brainwashing is in the eye of the beholder. When the outsider sees that the behavior, goals, and orientation of the Moonies have been so changed, he calls it brainwashing. I don't think I was brainwashed—just strongly influenced, manipulated by my own wanting to be acceptable, wanting to belong.

Two weeks ago, Mike and I were walking down the street together. Ahead we saw a neatly attired man and woman selling flowers and candy. Instantly we both recognized them as Moonies. They first approached Mike, asking, "Have you had your flower and Hershey bar today?" "No," Mike replied. "Would you like to buy some?" they asked. Mike responded in a matter-of-fact tone of voice, "No. I've already paid my dues to Rev. Sun Myung Moon." The couple was stunned, first stared at one another, then peered at us.

"You belong to the Unification Church, don't you?" asked Mike. They said nothing, only stared at him. A long, awkward minute passed. Mike repeated his question. They would not answer him. Finally the young man took the woman's hand and led her away. "They are protecting the Lord of the Second Advent," Mike explained. "It's still a secret. If people knew, they would persecute him the way they did Jesus." He smiled, held back a laugh, and said, "Having to protect the Lord—really!"

III. THE CHILDREN OF GOD

America is doomed. It is time to get out. Join us—we are the children of light. All others are the children of darkness.

Such is the message of the Children of God, the most radical of the profusion of contemporary cults. Once the most controversial of the Jesus freak sects, the Children of God have emerged as a permanent new religion with their own scriptures, prophet, and practices.

According to their elusive founder, Moses David (born David Brandt Berg), eight thousand Children of God missionaries are at work in eighty countries and have won two million converts. He claims that COG (the abbreviation by which the movement is widely known) is "the most explosive growth of a brand-new religious movement in history." [1]

A few years ago, they were as visible on the street corners

of America's major cities and college campuses as the devotees of Krishna. Today only a small portion of their three thousand U.S. converts remains in this country. The intervening years have seen them "scattered to the four corners of the earth, preaching doom to America, buttering up Libya's latter-day Caliph, Colonel Muammar Gaddafi and loosening up their sex ethics enough to lure

This envelope, one of several returned to the author from Children of God colonies in the United States and England, illustrates the problem of following the movement. During the past six years many of the colonies have left this country. Because of COG fear of deprogrammers and irate parents, the remaining American colonies have gone underground. Telephones have been disconnected and addresses changed. Without question, COG has abandoned the street corners of Berkeley, Los Angeles, and New York to the Hare Krishnas and the Moonies.

new members." They have evolved from a Fundamentalist salvation sect into "a brigade of international nomads." [2]

Like many other cults, COG believes that these are the last days, that contemporary events are the fulfillment of biblical prophecies concerning the end times. Again and again, Berg has seized upon political events in the Middle East, the land of prophecy, as signs of the end. Each time he has been wrong, but each time he has issued a fresh prediction. In 1973, he and the leaders of many sects viewed the approach of the comet Kohoutek as a sign of the impending destruction of the United States. In one of his many writings (called "Mo letters"), he exclaimed: *"You in the U.S. have only until January (1974) to get out of the States before some kind of disaster, destruction of judgment of God is to fall because of America's wickedness. . . . Now is the time! It's later than you think! Hallelujah! The End is near!"* COG disciples paraded the streets of every major city in the Western world wearing placards proclaiming, "Yet forty days and Nineveh shall be destroyed." A COG demonstration was held at the New York headquarters of the United Nations. Kohoutek was a fizzle—barely visible to the naked eye. No major disaster materialized. But the Children were not deterred. There are many, many signs yet to be seen.

Moses David and His Disciples

Who is Moses David? What is he like? He has lived in seclusion for eight years. Few of his disciples have ever seen him. He is not a particularly impressive or charismatic figure, but, from some remote part of the world, he is able to influence a worldwide movement through a profusion of "Mo letters"—at last five hundred of which have appeared to date. A former COG archbishop describes Berg as follows:

> He's in his mid-fifties [actually 59]. A frail man. He has a bad heart. He's got gray hair and sometimes wears a goatee. He has a large nose. And he has a strong face, strong features. He has piercing eyes, and when you meet him he seems like he's really checking you out. . . . Sometimes he rants and raves like a madman. Everybody is afraid of him.[3]

Who are the Children of God? What has drawn them to Berg and his message? When I visited the since abandoned Los Angeles headquarters of the Children of God in 1971, I found the members to be suspicious and hostile. When I tried talking to them I was subjected to a ruthless third degree about my religious experience, baptism, vocation, and church attendance. I parried with a barrage of questions of my own, demanding to know the very same things about my interrogators. A truce ensued. They allowed me to be shown around the grim warehouse in the skid row where they were housed and to meet several members even though the fact that I was not a "full-time gospel worker" distressed them. I found former drug addicts, ex-dope dealers, a rock musician, and an unwed mother—all typical Children. They hardly said anything other than Bible verses (frequently out of context) and "Hallelujah, brother."

COG as a Fundamentalist Sect

In 1971 COG was decidedly a Fundamentalist sect with pronounced emphases upon the need for personal salvation, the baptism of the Holy Spirit, reliance upon the Bible as the inspired Word of God—the only standard of faith and practice. COG was a community of obedience based upon a literal interpretation of Scripture, particularly the pentecostalism and communal sharing of the book of Acts. They were strict zealots interested only in convert-making. The two neon signs outside their headquarters read Jesus Saves and The Wages of Sin Is Death, But the Gift of God Is Eternal Life. Freeman Rogers of their revivalistic host organization, the Soul Clinic, described them well, "They became as radical for Christ as they once were for drugs, or sex, or the New Left." They were, Rogers insisted, so radical that they rejected all vocations except soul-winning, all earthly ties, all secular involvements, all compromise with the world, all halfway methods—even those of the most conservative Fundamentalists. New disciples were required to take a three-month course of basic training. They were then eligible for three additional sessions, which consisted of faultless memorization of scattered verses from the King James Version of the Bible.

COG gained notoriety for "using profane and vulgar language excessively, for demonstrating their hatred against 'the system' (disrupting church services . . .), and for requiring converts to . . . turn over all their possessions to the organization." [4] By 1972 they were on the enemies' list of every Jesus-movement group on the West Coast. They were openly accused of kidnapping, of being motivated by greed to seize the money and property of their converts, of using violence, of practicing hypnosis, of forcing young people to listen to their preaching by holding them against their will and depriving them of food and sleep. Soon the media joined the Fundamentalist groups in their suspicion of COG. And COG's archenemy, Ted Patrick, emerged. Charging that COG employed "brainwashing," Patrick countered by forcibly removing members of COG, detaining them against their will, in order to deprogram them on behalf of desperate parents.

The New Face of COG

Even before my visit to the Los Angeles location of COG, drastic changes had occurred in COG doctrine and morality, changes that had not yet filtered down to disciples on the local level. What had been a radical Fundamentalist sect with rather questionable attitudes toward the rights of individuals was about to become a totally unbiblical cult with equally questionable attitudes toward a host of practices.

In 1968 in Huntington Beach, California, David Berg undertook a ministry to young adult dropouts which would grow into "a globe-encircling network of 800 'colonies' [communes] in seventy countries. There are reportedly 5,000 full-time disciples, two-thirds of them male; fewer than 15 per cent are in the United States."[5] Swept along by the earthquake fever that struck California in 1968, Berg predicted an impending disaster, gathered his family and fifty or so converts into buses, and headed for the wilderness. His flock wandered from place to place in the Southwest, ekeing out a meager existence. The promised cataclysm never materialized, but the exodus of COG had welded them into a prophet-led people. It was at this time that COG found refuge with Fred Jordan's Soul Clinic. (Berg had once worked for Jordan.) Jordan used the colorful ex-hippies as evidence of the success of the gospel. In 1971 plans were shown to the author for a half-million-dollar colony (a ranch and truck farm) for which funds were being raised.

A distinct impression was given that COG was an outgrowth of Jordan's Soul Clinic like its many other enterprises. But Berg, his children, and in-laws were the mainstays and leaders of COG. The romance between Berg and Soul Clinic was a sometime thing. Jordan offered the Children sanctuary at the warehouse and at other of his properties and exploited them as a basis for his radio and television money-raising activities. But he at no time exercised any measure of control over COG. Finally their resistance to Jordan's authority and their deviation from the theology and techniques of the Soul Clinic led to a rupture. Shortly after my visit, COG was expelled from all Soul Clinic properties. COG left behind thousands of dollars in improvements, but during their sojourn their membership had grown from an initial fifty followers to more than fifteen hundred. A wandering band of ragged former hippies on the day they allied themselves with Jordan, they were a tightly organized, quasi-military shock force when they left Soul Clinic.

When COG was allied with Soul Clinic, they gave the Fundamentalist image I have described. To avoid legal complications, they claimed that they would not accept members who were less than legal age. Incoming members were required to sell all their possessions and donate the proceeds to the movement. "You have to understand," Freeman Rogers explained, "these young people get as high on religion as they formerly got on drugs. Most of them were freaked out of their minds before the Children found them; they had come to the end of the road. So when the Children asked them to give up everything and follow Christ, they really had nothing to lose." But even an automobile and a small bank account amount to something, particularly when multiplied by a few thousand. All members were given new, biblical names such as Sarah, Isaac, and Martha. Their lives were strictly regulated, ascetic: no drugs, no sex outside of marriage, no outside work of any kind, no contact with parents or former friends except for the purpose of witnessing to them. Every minute of the day was tightly scheduled. No one was ever left alone. Children traveled in groups. Privacy was never allowed. From reveille at 6:45 A.M. until lights-out at 11:30 P.M., the day was spent in manual labor, household chores, Bible study, worship, street witnessing, memorizing and reciting scriptures, and praying.

But as early as 1969 the direction of COG had been fundamentally altered. A crisis had occurred in the life of David Berg. Berg was married but was living with his secretary, Maria, and word was leaking out. In the words of Jack Wasson (Brother Timotheus) who is married to one of the original Huntington Beach members: "David Berg was doing what was explicitly forbidden by Scripture, and he knew it. To justify himself, he had to come up with something that was at least as authoritative as Scripture if not more so." The answer was the first "Mo letter," *The Old Church and the New Church*. Berg had received a prophecy telling him that the Bible was the inspired Word of God for *yesterday,* and the "Mo letters" are the inspired word of God for *today.* God had revealed that Maria was the new church and Jane Berg, his wife, was the old church. God was putting Jane aside because she was a hindrance to his work. And in her place, God was giving Berg a new wife, Maria.

The Old Church and the New Church not only solved Berg's personal problem, it established his voice as that of a divine oracle, answerable only to God. No one could question his authority without being excommunicated. But even more than this, Berg had hit upon a scheme to enrich himself and finance his movement—the sale of the "Mo letters." As we have noted, to date there have been more than five hundred letters. Each is sent out to the colonies where it is sold on the streets. As Wasson explains:

> Copies are sent to area leaders, who print them up for the colonies. COG headquaters formerly got $.25 royalty per disciple on each letter as it was issued. But now at least 40 per cent of all the money the kids make on the street "litnessing" is sent to higher administrative levels. According to a recent issue of the *New Nation News* (the official COG news publication), 218,108,922 MO letters were distributed in a 4¼-year period beginning October 1, 1971, which breaks down to approximately 4.3 million per month.[6]

Further Wasson relates the average donation per letter is between five cents and a dollar. An American colony would produce between five hundred and a thousand dollars a day. COG also runs discotheques that charge admission fees. Jack continues: "They put their slogans on coffee cups and sell little gold yokes and MO tee shirts with COG slogans. . . . They're marketing tapes and albums."[7] Income is also derived from converts who "forsake all," as well as from friends and parents of converts. Berg contends that such funds can sustain COG indefinitely. In addition, merchants are approached for food, lodgings, goods, and services with the hard-sell pitch: "We're a Christian group. We're trying to help kids off drugs. If you can help us out, we'll really appreciate it and God will bless you."[8] But, in reality, there is no drug program of any kind.

Within the COG colonies, the "Mo letters" are considered superior to the Bible. As Berg proclaimed in the 1973 letter *Old Bottles:*

> I want to frankly tell you, if there is a choice between reading your Bible, I want to tell you that you better read what God said today, in preference to what he said 2,000 and 4,000 years ago. Then when you've gotten done reading the latest MO letters, you can go back to reading the Bible.[9]

In the early days of COG, the Bible and only the Bible was authoritative. David Jacks, who held important posts within the COG international structure during his five years as a disciple, reports: "I am convinced that in the early days most members were born again and really received Jesus as their personal Saviour when they entered the group. Salvation verses were really stressed—John 3:16, Romans 10:9,10, Romans 3:23 and 6:23, John 1:12, Revelation 3:20, and so on."[10] I recall the Children's recitation of these favorite revivalistic texts together with passages pertaining to the baptism of the Spirit and speaking in tongues. I remember the singsong, rote incantation of these Bible verses. They were like computers programmed with a limited number of responses. It made little difference what the recited text meant—just so it was from the Bible. It is not too difficult for me to conceive of the Children's accepting Berg's usurpation of the function of divine prophet, particularly because he could always find a prooftext from the Bible for justification.

"He [Berg] definitely believes he is God's endtime prophet," comments former disciple Wasson. "He believes he is the fulfillment of those Old Testament messages which refer to King David, who was to come in the future. . . . Obviously, comparing himself to King David and Moses serves very nicely for his pyramid type of leadership structure, with penalties for disobedience to God's endtime leader." It is the disciple's duty to obey without question. To entertain the slightest doubt or reservation about Berg's leadership is an act of rebellion against God that will be judged by God. Wasson adds, "The result of this sort of indoctrination is a reign of terror." [11] For the disciple becomes dependent upon the teachings of the prophet, distrustful of his own reason, afraid that he will fall from divine grace by questioning Berg's teachings. Further, he knows from experience that should he voice any objection, he will be ostracized by the colony, cut off from his only friends, cast out onto the streets with nothing but the clothes on his back.

COG Joins the Sexual Revolution

Once Berg had hurdled his own sexual inhibitions, divine permission for his disciples quickly followed. Four years ago, *Time* magazine reported: "COG Evangelists are preaching a sexual-freedom line unusual for the Jesus movement. Masturbation and pre-marital sex, for example, are now only sinful if indulged in 'too much' like hiking, swimming, or exercising too much. Polygamy is also condoned though not recommended."[12] The top leadership were having affairs with members. Berg was citing the example of Abraham, Solomon, and David to justify "having concubines." "Mo letters" increasingly turned into "fundamentalist pornography." *Mountain Maid* devotes three hundred lines of ridiculous doggerel to urging women to bare their breasts. A sample line:

> Can't we leave those summits bare
> without all that underwear?

Mate-swapping was encouraged under the doctrine that members are to hold "all things common," Acts 2:44 being cited as a prooftext (or pretext!).

In a 1974 "Mo letter" *God's Love Slave!* Berg describes how he offered his wife, Maria, to numerous men. In *Flirty Little Fishy,* also published in 1974, Berg encourages fornication for the purpose of winning converts. A mermaid is pictured making love to a naked man. The caption reads "Hooker for Jesus." Mass-circulation magazines in the United States and Germany have reported that COG maintains a school on the estate of an Italian duke where attractive females are trained in the art of seduction.[13] Venereal disease and pregnancy among unwed mothers are common.

As in previous years, all marriages must be approved by COG leadership, but marriage itself is under attack by Berg. In *One Wife* he declares:

> God breaks up marriages in order that he might join each of the parties together to himself. He rips off wives, husbands, or children to make up his bride if the rest of the family refuses to follow. He is the worst "ripper-offer" of all. God is the greatest destroyer of home and family of anybody! . . . If you have not forsaken your husband or wife for the Lord at some time or another, you have not forsaken all.[14]

Other "Mo letters" record Berg's communications with the spirits of the departed, his "spiritual counselors" who include Abrahim (a gypsy king), Rasputin, Joan of Arc, the Pied Piper, Oliver Cromwell, William Jennings Bryan, Merlin the Magician, and Martin Luther. *Jesus and Sex* commends intoxication as a means of yielding to God's spirit. In *Madame M* Berg tells of visiting a fortune-teller at the time his son Paul ("Aaron" in COG) fell or jumped to his death in the Alps. *Revolutionary Love Making* details Jesus' sexual relationships with the women who followed him. *Women in Love* reasserts the biblical condemnation of male homosexuality but recommends lesbianism.

The Enemies of COG

In the summer of 1977 an apparently spurious "Mo letter," *God Bless You—And: Good-Bye!* was distributed. In this letter, Moses David admits that he has been a "false prophet." It is announced that the Children of God movement "has come to an end now and forever." Moses David confesses to having misled his flock, palming off his own thoughts as those of God. In response, a tape recording of "the *real* Moses David" was distributed by Barbara Canevaro ("Queen Rachel") who claims that she is Berg's "official representative . . . authorized to speak for him in all matters." The voice on the tape denounces the letter as "nothing but a completely fraudulent and lying forgery, rather shabbily concocted by some crackpot who is apparently partially demented." It demonstrates, the voice continues, "what slimy stinking depths our enemies do not hesitate to slither to try to stop us, including criminal acts of kidnapping, involuntary incarceration, mental and physical torture and even murder!"[15]

Assuming that it is Berg who speaks in the recorded message, there is great irony in his reference to the harassment and persecution that COG has endured. It was not so long ago that COG was accused of a similar list of offenses. From the beginning, COG has resorted to acts of violence, theft, and abuse. They have seized the property of at least one other sect, justifying the act as "taking spoils from the Gentiles" in the manner practiced by the wandering tribes of Israel during their conquest of the Promised Land. They have often practiced intimidation. A favorite tactic of COG has been to drift into a church service, fifty or sixty strong in full hippie regalia, and to occupy the first rows of pews as well as to sit on the floor in aisles in the area between the first row and the pulpit. Their very presence could disrupt a church service. If they were welcomed by the pastor and congregation, they would interrupt the service with questions and biblical quotations intended to create confusion. Should the ensuing discussion become heated, they have been known to resort to "smiting" their enemies, that is, striking them over the head with a Bible. The most dramatic of their attention-getting devices have been the "vigils." According to one observer:

> As the Spirit leads, the "Prophets of Doom" . . . don red sackcloth (symbol of mourning), place wooden yokes about their necks (symbol of willingness to be a "slave of love" to Christ). Carrying wooden staves (symbol of divine judgment), they stand in protest at public meetings, to denounce the unrepentant. Imagine the stunning impact when Jerry Rubin came to the campus of the University of California at Santa Barbara to make a speech! In marched a long line of sackcloth-and-ashes-garbed youth, staves and signs in hand, who stood stone faced and silent. At a signal the whole line began to clank the staves on the pavement in unison and chant, "Woe, Woe, Woe, Woe, Woe." Rubin never had a chance.[16]

Their evangelistic techniques are among the most coercive that I have ever witnessed. The following account accurately depicts the COG style of convert-making:

> A nursing student in Los Angeles was downtown shopping for shoes when she was confronted by some of the Children of God. She was nervous and tense at the time, aggravated by the fact that she could not find shoes that suited her. The

Children said to her, "Why don't you come and live with us? We don't worry about needing to get shoes. We have plenty of shoes and plenty of everything else that we need."[17]

The product of a Christian home, the student was encouraged by the Children to come with them to the colony to talk further. When she began to hesitate, she was told that this was because the devil was urging her to resist. After a lengthy discussion liberally seasoned with familiar biblical texts, she gave in and went with them. At the colony, the Children

> tried to talk the student nurse into selling all her belongings and giving them the money. When she asked if she could go home and talk to her parents about joining them, they urged her not to communicate with them at all. "Let the dead bury the dead," they said. She asked when she could see her parents if she decided to stay. They told her that they would send her to . . . .Texas . . . for a few months, and after that she would return to Los Angeles. Only then could she communicate with her parents, if she wanted to. But they thought that by that time she would probably have no desire to do so.[18]

Confused and shaken, she indicated that she desired to postpone her decision and wanted to leave. The Children responded by forming a circle around her and

> started praying loudly for her, asking that the Lord would take away all her belongings so that she would see that she was supposed to stay. However, when she absolutely insisted on leaving, they finally allowed her to go.[19]

What had led her to visit the Children in the first place? A deep sense of guilt stemming from the fact that she was not living in accordance with the dictates of the Christian faith in which she had been reared. Her heavy drinking and drug use required some sacrifice in order to restore equilibrium to her troubled soul. The Children had preyed upon her dread and uncertainty. They had placed her in a context in which she was subjected to nonstop indoctrination. After several hours of being bombarded with Bible verses, prayers, personal testimonies of miraculous conversion, threats of damnation, she was even more confused. After all, the Bible, prayer, and conversion were all "holy things" in the family situation in which she had spent her childhood. And these "holy things" fascinated and attracted her, even though the COG mode of presentation was foreign to her background.

Their aggressive techniques and their eagerness to whisk converts away from their families and friends led the other evangelistic groups of the Jesus movement to denounce the Children of God, accusing them of engaging in kidnapping, holding young people against their will, depriving them of food and sleep, and hypnotizing them into submission. I have always felt that the critics of COG overstated their case, but there has been enough truth to such objections to warrant extreme caution in dealing with the Children.

Distraught parents have been entirely in agreement with the Jesus movement's denunciations of COG. "My child did not voluntarily forsake the way of life and values that we instilled in him (or her)," they have argued. "He (or she) must have been brainwashed. I cannot accept the fact that I have failed as a parent; therefore I will do something to save my child—whatever the cost." Out of such desperation deprogramming was born. With almost total impunity, Ted Patrick and his associates have been abducting Children of God from their colonies, subjecting them to a forced counterconversion as excessive and coercive as any COG effort at soul-winning. Patrick has been successful more often than not. But serious moral questions remain about the propriety of abridging an individual's civil rights because he or she adopts a life-style repugnant to parents or friends.

More than any other cult, COG has been the object of the deprogrammers. In the opinion of the author, Patrick's interference with their freedom of action has been as instrumental in their leaving the country as any prophecy of impending destruction. The deprogrammers may have won a few hundred back, but they have driven thousands to foreign lands and have provided the confirmation of faith that only sustained persecution produces. Left to themselves, probably the same percentage of Children would have fallen away from the movement as have been coerced into subjection by deprogramming.

And what is the future of the Children of God? Can Berg maintain his control of the scattered colonies? Will some of the older, more Fundamentalist leadership persuade disciples to repudiate the "Mo letters" and return to the Bible? What will happen when Berg passes from the scene? Frankly, it is amazing that COG has endured this long. The persistence of COG surely attests to the deep needs felt by its disciples more than it does to the magnetism of its prophet-founder. Some commentators feel that a permanent religious movement has arisen, that we are witnessing the development of another Church of Jesus Christ of Latter Day Saints. For just as the Mormons have prospered despite the sexual weakness of their early leadership, abuses of power within, persecution from without, the murder of their founder, schisms, and self-imposed exile, so it may be that COG has completed the first decade of what may be a long history.

IV. HARE KRISHNA!

My wife and I have just returned from Krishna's birthday party. It was held at the Sri Sri Radha Krishna Temple in Berkeley, about a mile from the University of California. There was singing and dancing, a parade with a horse-drawn chariot and a brass band, a fifteen-course vegetarian feast as well as a fire sacrifice, a Vedic wedding ceremony, and rites of initiation!

We were only forty minutes from home; yet I felt as though I were Cary Grant in *Gunga Din* wandering about in a Hindu temple. But the only Indians present were visitors, and all the temple residents were healthy, cheerful-looking young Americans. But they were not Americans exactly. After all, the clothes and the makeup were more Calcutta than California, the language was

Initiation at ISKCON temple, Berkeley, California. (Photo by author.)

often Sanskrit, and what they were doing was decidedly *not* something that would be permitted at the First Baptist Church in Maywood, Illinois.

Imagine a large white stucco and marble building (once a Mormon temple!), resplendent in gold, sky blue, and flaming red. Imagine half-naked temple attendants wafting incense with peacock plumes and bowing in adoration before images of alien dieties. Picture a service called to order by the sounding of a conch shell as barefooted worshipers throw their bodies to the floor, prostrate themselves before Krishna, "the Supreme Personality of Godhead." Think of a ceremony that returns again and again to the chanting of the "great mantra": *Hare Krishna, Hare Krishna, Krishna, Krishna, Hare Hare; Hare Rama, Hare Rama, Rama, Rama, Hare Hare.* Think of devotees imploring you to forget the world of passing fancies and to renew your dormant state of God consciousness. Join them, if but for a moment, and free yourself from anxiety as you enter into pure, unending, blissful consciousness.

We watched as a young couple, scarcely older than my college-aged son and daughter, were joined in marriage. We heard them take vows that no American couple of our acquaintance would exchange: The male is to be totally dominant and responsible; the woman is to be completely submissive and obedient. They will come together as man and wife only one day a month for the purpose of conceiving Krishna-conscious children. All their actions will be offerings to Krishna. Their lives will be lived for him—not for each other. Nothing will be done for sense gratification. Nothing will be done for security and family. In time, they may even go their separate ways as wandering hermits, seeking Krishna, and Krishna alone.

I was amazed by the material prosperity of the temple with its exotic carvings, statuary, and artifacts. I was impressed by the seventy earnest devotees who resided there, who daily launch out into the cruel materialistic world seeking converts and cash for Krishna. I had previously met many of them on the streets of San Francisco's Fisherman's Wharf, at the airport, and on the Berkeley campus. I was struck by the fact that no one was more than twenty-nine (though tiny children were numerous). Yet I wondered why it was that in the seven years since I first visited a temple of Krishna, I have never met a devotee much beyond his or her twenties. Suddenly, I thought of a more recent motion picture, *Logan's Run,* and of the domed city where life ended at thirty in a ritual of fire.

This, then, suggests my basic question to the devotees of Krishna on the celebration of *Janmastami,* the day of the appearance of Lord Krishna: Has your life begun, or has it ended?

Joy and wonder are basic to life iself. No religious movement can be described as a living faith that does not find room for states of ecstasy. For devotees of Krishna, the central act of being is achieving bliss by chanting the Hare Krishna mantra. In temples throughout the world and on streets of dozens of cities, the timeless names of Krishna and His Divine Energy resound. According to devotees, the words of the mantra are not ordinary words but transcendental sound vibrations, a linking of the individual with the divine power present in all things. Chanting the great mantra without ceasing, losing oneself in total bliss, finding a high that lasts forever—this is what Krishna Consciousness is all about. Everything else is insignificant.

The power of the cosmic vibrations loosed by chanting influence not only the chanter but ripple outward throughout the world. *Sankirtana,* or public chanting, is just as important as chanting in Krishna's holy places. Sankirtana parties consisting of all the members of a given temple, except those assigned to cook the evening meal, daily head for community crossroads equipped with bottles of drinking water, food, wire racks of literature, and other necessary accoutrements.

Krishna's birthday parade. Berkeley, California.

At their destination, the majority of the party stands in a row and chants. One devotee holds aloft a poster of Lord Krishna, while others accompany the chant with *mrdanga,* a drum, and *karatals,* small cymbals. The mantra is sung in ever-increasing tempo, the devotees weave back and forth in a simple two-step that increases in intensity until it reaches a peak of fervor and frenzy. Even at its emotional summit the experience is highly stylized. There is never a deviation, never a spontaneous utterance, never an act of embracing, running, falling, or jumping. Only the mantra, the exclamation *"Hare bol!"* ("Chant the holy name") or a violent shudder accompanied by the slow enunciation of the name *Krishna* are heard.

While drums boom, cymbals clink, and the chanters are transported to ecstatic heights; other devotees mingle with the curious onlookers, attempting to sell literature or to engage individuals in conversation. If a passer-by shows

Photo by Glen A. Pierce.

Hare Krishnas soliciting contributions near the temple in Germantown, Pennsylvania.

interest and wants to know about the group and its beliefs, he is handed a printed card bearing the Hare Krishna mantra and the address of the temple.

The physical appearance of Krishna's devotees makes them quite visible as they chant the Hare Krishna mantra on the street corners of major cities and univerity towns. The men shave their heads except for a tuft of hair high on the back of the scalp. This tuft, or *sikha,* is a centuries-old sign of devotion of Krishna.

The men wear the *dhoti,* a cloth wrapped around the

waist and tied either at the shoulder or the waist. Women wear the *sari,* a one-piece garment wrapped around the body and over the top of the head. The sari is worn over a blouse-type garment. Unmarried men and women wear saffron-colored garments, while the married devotees wear yellow. (Because of difficulties in obtaining the proper colored cloth, the colors are sometimes interchanged.) Tennis shoes or sandals are usually worn in the streets, but many devotees chant barefooted.

Each devotee adorns his or her body with *tilak,* fuller's earth mixed with water. Two parallel lines, a sign of devotion to Krishna, are applied in exact order to the forehead, navel, chest, throat, right waist, right forearm, right shoulder, left waist, left forearm, left shoulder, between the shoulder blades, and lower back. Each devotee wears a string of 108 *japa* beads in a bag hung around the neck. The beads are used in the manner of a rosary for chanting the Hare Krishna mantra—sixteen rounds on the beads being required each day. Very little jewelry is worn; some of the women favor Indian earrings in pierced earlobes as well as nose jewelry.

Anatomy of a Krishna Convert

Who becomes a Hare Krishna convert? The impressions of the typical Krishna devotee that I jotted down after initial conversations with about a dozen temple residents in Philadelphia were as follows: they are quite young, have little ego strength, little imagination, almost no ambition. They are college dropouts with a liberal arts background, usually in English literature, theater, etc. They come from lower–middle-class homes mostly in the Boston to Washington urban corridor. They are oldest or middle children, have been alienated from their parents for years.

No devotee has ever given the slightest indication of having felt close to a parent or a brother or a sister. Yet they have spent very little time *not* under their parents' roof before joining the movement. They are slightly depressed, dependent, and nervous. Most of them seem completely asexual, very unsure of their sexual identity. I would emphasize that this description is highly impressionistic. A more accurate profile based on a questionnaire study reveals that the typical Krishna devotee is American, male, single, white, twenty-two and a half years old, a high school graduate, of nominal Protestant background, has lived in a temple for a year, is not an initiated member but has been recommended for and expects initiation soon. There is a fifty-fifty chance that this typical devotee has been a regular user of psychedelic drugs but not heroin. His last drug experience was a little over a year ago. Before his conversion he had gone through an intensive search for the purpose and meaning of life. His decision to move into a Krishna Consciousness temple was made less than two years after his first contact with the movement. His parents, middle-class in income and attitude, are not pleased with his conversion and have attempted to dissuade him from continuing. At the same time, they are happier with his present life-style than they were with his former behavior, his hippie attitudes, especially his drug use.

Lou, a student of mine at Temple University in the mid sixties, was the first devotee I had met. He and his wife, Holly, lived in a rambling apartment in Germantown, a once-fashionable, now down-at-the-heels integrated community a few miles from the university campus in Philadelphia. They had very few possessions: an ancient sofa, a few beds, cribs for their two tiny children, a beat-up portable phonograph, books, phonograph records, a refrigerator, and stove. They were food faddists and, above all, "heads." Lou and Holly were known as unfailing sources of high-grade pot and hash.

I valued my acquaintance with them because nothing that was happening in the counterculture passed them by. When the rock scene was heavily into drugs, Lou and Holly were heavily into drugs. When the Beatles began investigating Eastern spirituality, Lou and Holly began to investigate Eastern spirituality. By the time George Harrison had recorded "My Sweet Lord," Lou and Holly were attending the Philadelphia temple of Krishna Consciousness and chanting the Hare Krishna mantra.

The last time I was in touch with them, Lou was known as Rabindra and was serving as president of Krishna temple. His appearance had changed drastically—as one would imagine. He bore a striking resemblance to Mahatma Gandhi. As for Holly, the transition from jeans to sari was not too dramatic. Their children were about to depart for the Krishna school in Texas.

There was something disconcerting about their children, especially three-year-old Julia, whom I had known since her birth. Here was a Shirley Temple look-alike with blonde curly hair and large, expressive eyes costumed as an Indian villager, talking to me, her parents, other adults, and children as though the only world was the realm of Krishna. And for her—unlike her parents who had renounced middle-class comforts and countercultural struggle alike—Krishna was all.

Yoga Maya

I have always found the devotees of Krishna approachable, eager to share their experiences. Their temples are open to outsiders. Leftover *prasadam* (food that has been ceremonially dedicated to Krishna) is always shared with those in need of a meal. (They are doing more than feeding you, of course. They are—without your knowledge—causing you to participate in the worship of Krishna by consuming that which is his.) Let me describe Yoga Maya as representative of the dozens with whom the author and others have spoken.[1]

A middle-aged couple stood at the door of the New York temple, asking to see someone. The woman was evidently in a state of agitation. "We are Evelyn's parents, and we want to see Evelyn." Three or four devotees began clustering around the door. "Yoga Maya is upstairs," Gour Hari das, the temple treasurer, responded and dispatched a devotee to bring her down. "Yoga Maya—yes, that's what you call her. Her name is Evelyn!" retorted the woman.

A first-class hassle ensued involving Evelyn's mother and the devotees. A heated discussion to the accompaniment of chanting made it progressively more difficult for everyone to carry on a conversation.

Later the same afternoon, Evelyn, or Yoga Maya, was alone in the temple's art gallery. She was eager to tell her story. Evelyn was born twenty-six years ago in New York State. Her father is a court stenographer. She was raised in a conservative Jewish home where religion was taken very seriously. She was graduated from the State University at Buffalo with a degree in English. Then she married and moved to San Francisco, teaching high school English in the local school system for a year and a half. Subsequently she left her husband and moved to Marin County, lived with a group of friends, and began taking drugs. "For six months," she says, "I didn't do much—just trying to enjoy."

Several in the Marin County group turned revolutionary, including Evelyn. She relates, "The injustice and suffering around us frustrated us." Leaving northern California, she went to the Hawaiian island of Maui.

> I continued to question my values and my life. I couldn't go back to teaching. I wanted to teach, but I wanted to teach the truth and didn't know it. So I started reading various scriptures and got into impersonal philosophy and various forms of yoga. Simultaneously, I was chanting the Hare Krishna mantra. The devotees had weekend feasts on Maui, and I was attracted by the chanting and the night's prasadam. In a short time the chant took over everything else. I gave up yoga and stopped reading the Bible and books on Zen. I kept on reading the *Bhagavad-Gita.* I made a very quick decision one night, to give away most of my things and to move into the temple in Honolulu. I thought to myself, "I will give myself one month"—an experiment. I wanted to be open to the process—to see what Krishna Consciousness was all about. That was December of 1970. It was a very big adjustment. But the process of spiritual self-realization is gradual. You make advancement in relation to the degree of surrender. I was convinced in a few days, and since then, I have never wavered. There is no possibility of wavering, unless you stop breathing and chanting, then you could forget.
>
> I had a difficult time at first. . . . All I was doing was washing pots and going on sankirtana [street chanting] parties. So I came to New York. Here I began teaching the children of devotees and also got involved in editing Srila Prabhupada's books.

She is now married to someone in the movement and is expecting a "devoted child." She added, "I'm starting to see and hear things properly—in proper perspective in relation to God."

Her family remains a sensitive topic. "I've had little contact with them over the past ten years," she stated. "Since I have been in the temple here, they've come about once a month. They don't like Krishna Consciousness because they don't understand. My sister, thirty, won't listen and won't read the literature. My brother, twenty-two, is a little more receptive."

She volunteered the information that she had obtained a divorce the previous week. "Up to then my husband sent me money from time to time, and I would send him Krishna books." Obviously she had been married to a devotee and had become pregnant by him before receiving a divorce from her former husband. She continued: "Since I joined Krishna Consciousness, it's been so peaceful—transcendent from anxiety—removed from suffering. I am happy; especially about having a baby. My husband is an artist. He's lived in the temple for four years. The marriage was arranged by the temple president. We had a nice fire sacrifice at the wedding, here in the New York temple. Several were married at the same time."

Stay high forever! Tune in! Drop out! End all downers! Find a life that is peaceful, free from anxiety, removed from suffering. Be happy. And the cost? A life that is ordered and structured and *arranged*.

What exactly is Krishna Consciousness? What are the rules? What or who does the arranging?

ISKCON

ISKCON, the International Society of Krishna Consciousness, is the American manifestation of an ancient Hindu sect whose doctrine and ritual were brought to the United States by A. C. Bhaktivedanta in September, 1965. Formally incorporated in July of the following year, ISKCON has attracted tens of thousands of Americans—especially young adults. A religion of worship and grace rather than of mystic contemplation and yogic discipline, Krishna Consciousness now numbers more than two thousand devotees in nearly forty temples throughout the United States. The world headquarters and the ISKCON publishing house are in Los Angeles. There are also several centers in Europe, Africa, Latin America, the South Seas, and Asia.

Devotion to the Lord Krishna is a total way of life requiring the adoption by the initiate of a new name, an Indian manner of dress, a strict code of behavior governing every aspect of existence—diet, marriage, family life, vocation, etc. The International Society for Krishna Consciousness is a Hindu sect following the principles of *bhakti,* the path of devotion to a personal diety. The bhakti cults of India express their faith in love and adoration of a god or gods. As K. M. Sen notes, this approach to Hindu life "has not been much concerned with the intricacies of theology, . . . God is here looked upon as an intensely lovable Creator, and the *Bhakti* movement led to religious exuberance rather than to calm speculations."[2] Although abstract, mystical Hinduism is better known in the West; bhakti is much more the everyday religion of India. Most people native to India are Hindus, and most Hindus are the devotees of a particular deity such as Vishnu, Shiva, or one of Shiva's consorts (e.g., Kali or Durga). According to Hindu mythology, Vishnu the redeemer appears in human history in the form of an *avatar* whenever the world is in peril. His principle avatars are Prince Rama (the legendary hero whose struggles to regain his throne and beloved wife are recounted in the *Ramayana*), the Buddha, and, of course, Krishna, the "paramount deity of Hindu worship." The character of Krishna is quite complex, for his cult has absorbed into it many legends, traditions, and disciplines. On the one hand, there is the mischievous infant hero, content to manifest his great powers as a god in childish pranks. Then there is Krishna among the *gopis* (goatherd girls), an erotic figure whose sexual relations, particularly with his beloved Radha, are symbols of the union of the human soul with the divine. Above all, there is Krishna in the form of Arjuna's left-handed bowman and charioteer, explaining to the great warrior on the eve of a fratricidal battle all that a Hindu need know concerning life, death, duty, and destiny. It is here in the pages of the *Bhagavad-Gita,* the "layman's Bible of Hinduism," that Krishna reveals that he is a manifestation of the abstract One, the universal Spirit that is beyond all distinctions.

The many gods of the Hindu pantheon, Krishna included, are seen as but aspects which the fertility of the Absolute assumes in its desire to project itself into innumerable forms. The world of the senses and even the gods themselves are *maya,* or illusion. They are the divine Spirit at play with itself. Yet by worshiping any one of the gods, be it Krishna or Vishnu or Shiva or Durga, by losing oneself in the ecstasy of music and dancing, the individual psyche breaks away from its boundaries and returns to the divine Spirit, the Source from which all beings have emerged.

The ISKCON Way of Life

The purpose of ISKCON is to awaken the world "to the normal, ecstatic state of Krishna Consciousness." Disciples are not required to grasp difficult religious truths or engage in austere exercises. As one temple resident says: "All this talk about temple life and the meaning of the various rituals is *maya*—illusion. It will pass away. It is nothing. Only chanting the Hare Krishna *mantra* is useful." In order to restore all men to their "eternal position of favorably serving the will of Krishna," ISKCON's adherents engage in public chanting, the publishing and distribution of books, records, periodicals, etc., and maintain local temples for public instruction and worship.

Our lengthiest investigations were conducted at temples in Philadelphia and Berkeley. Among the members, there are several distinct levels or degrees of involvement in temple activities. The least involved is the individual who encounters a sankirtana party on the streets. If he participates in any way, even by indicating his enjoyment of the chant, it is believed that he is at the moment worshiping Krishna. The next level of involvement is the individual who visits the temple, witnesses or participates in the chanting and dancing, and partakes of the public meal served on Sunday. Serious commitment to the movement begins when a person chants at home or at work and installs an altar in his house. The worshiper offers food and may even adopt the schedule and dress of the temple residents.

The next step is to join the temple and to move in. Both single persons and married couples are welcome. After about three months, one is eligible for initiation. The temple president must write a letter of recommendation to His Divine Grace Srila Prabhupada. If His Divine Grace happens to visit the local temple, the initiation may be done by him in person—an especially auspicious occasion in a devotee's life. Otherwise word is received by mail confirming the initiation of the devotee. Only Srila Prabhupada can initiate a devotee. When I visited a temple in 1972, only the temple president and his wife and a new arrival from New York were full initiates. Several others had been recommended, but approval had not been received. It can take several months. When initiated, a single man is known as a *brahmin,* and a single woman as a *brahmacharin.*

The final stage of assent for the devotee during his present earthy lifetime is that of *sannyasa,* or wandering holy person. At this point the individual no longer attaches himself to any one location but spends his life wandering from temple to temple. Srila Prabhupada attained sannyasa in 1959.

A Temple Ceremony

At the temple, the *aratrika* ceremony is the most common religious rite—the ceremony in which Krishna is presented offerings of food, incense, flowers, a waving handkerchief, a fan, water, or flames. A Sunday aratrika that I attended went as follows. At 4:00 P.M. everyone made an offering of rice before the seat of His Divine Grace A. C. Bhaktivedanta Swami Prabhupada. Then for thirty minutes everyone chanted the Hare Krishna mantra responsively—one person chanting the first phrase, the group responding with the next phrase, and so forth. This was done with clapping and dancing, to the accompaniment of an electric chord organ, a mrdanga, several pairs of karatals, two tambourines, and some wooden and metal clappers. After the chanting, the devotees bowed and responsively recited while prostrating themselves in obeisance, while two devotees continued to stand as they again chanted the mantra, this time for only a few minutes. Once again, all bowed in obeisance.

Next the temple president gave a twenty-minute lecture. Although he is an American, born and reared in New Jersey, he talks in an Indian singsong, as do most of the long-term devotees. The lecture is presented only at the

Sunday feast. First he welcomed the guest, giving a brief history of ISKCON in which he stressed the importance of the *Bhagavad-Gita,* bhakti yoga, and the Hare Krishna mantra. He spoke of the grace of Srila Prabhupada, saying that at first devotees were required to chant sixty-four rounds daily on the japa beads ($64 \times 108 = 6{,}912$ mantras per day). This being too much for American devotees, His Divine Grace reduced it to thirty-two rounds per day, but even this was too great a requirement; so "in his infinite mercy and wisdom" he reduced the requirement to sixteen rounds ($16 \times 108 = 1{,}728$ mantras per day).

The leader read a precept from the *Gita,* and then delivered a short homily on it. Then he would read the next quote, giving thoughts on it, so on, and so forth. All of his material was derived virtually word for word from the teaching of Srila Prabhupada as found in *Back to Godhead* magazine. Occasionally he would ask questions, catechetical in nature, with the answer virtually given in the question. For example, the leader was expounding on the futility of activity, be it good or bad. He asked for an illustration. The leader's wife responded: "Giving one hundred dollars to a beggar is not good. The beggar must come back in a later life to pay you back, and you must be reincarnated to receive his repayment." The obvious moral: Do no works of charity—a philosophy that seems to pervade the life-style of Krishna devotees, who renounce "practical work" in the "mundane world" as utter foolishness.

The president continued by saying that it is not necessary to live in the temple to be a true devotee of Krishna. The individual should build a temple at home. He could follow much of the same routine as that of the temple, rising at the same time (3:30 A.M.) and offering food to Krishna. If he could not afford to install deities in his home, then he could simply chant the Hare Krishna mantra. He instructed his audience that they should support the local temple with their gifts and should attend the feasts. Also they should be careful to associate only with devotees and should avoid unbelievers. After the message, everyone stood and chanted the mantra for ten minutes. This time the music and dancing were more exuberant than during the earlier chanting.

At 5:10 P.M. the tray of food to be offered was brought in, strangely covered with aluminum foil. The food was offered at the altar with incense, a fan, water, flame, and a conch shell. The flame was carried through the assembled devotees, each one passing his hand over it and then touching his forehead. The water was likewise carried about, each person being sprinkled. Throughout the offering ceremonies the ministrant rang a small temple bell. At 5:40 P.M. the aratrika was over, concluded with the blowing of a conch shell and obeisance. The temple president then asked the visitors to consider membership in the temple.

While the aratrika was being performed, four female devotees were in the prasadam room, placing servings of food on paper plates and arranging them on the floor at the end of the room. When the ceremony concluded, the visitors and devotees went into the prasadam room, and each picked up a plate and a styrofoam cup of water. There were no utensils. Since the crowd was large, some went into the library to eat while others found a spot on the floor in the prasadam room. The devotees were careful to speak with all visitors about Krishna Consciousness, not allowing any of us to sit alone for more than a few minutes at a time. As I ate, I was visited by at least half of the temple residents. The feast continued for an hour. The meal was completely vegetarian—milk, fruits, vegetables, grains, sugar, and honey. It is not, however, health food. No attempt is made to obtain only organically grown food or to avoid bleached flour or chemical additives. I found the various dishes, all of which are prepared according to Indian recipes, quite tasty but much more like dessert or baby food than a main meal. In the kitchen I noticed a rack of commercial vitamin supplements including Vitamin C, Korval Multiple Vitamins with Iron, and Flintstone Vitamins with Iron. (The claim is made by critics that the meatless diet of the devotees is deficient in protein and other essential nutrients.)

After the feast, we were entertained by a play depicting passages from the Sanskrit scriptures. The production that featured the temple initiates in makeup and masks depicting witches, wizards, legendary heroes, and gods was altogether crude and amateurish. I was reminded of the purely literalistic tableaus often performed by church Sunday school programs, e.g., the perennial nativity plays at Christmastime.

Temple Organization

Each local temple is directed by a president who is responsible for making all decisions and arranging the temple schedule. The average president is twenty-five and has been a devotee for three years. The president stands in the stead of Srila Prabhupada. Second in leadership is the temple commander, who assigns household duties to the devotees including cleaning, flower arranging, shopping, painting, the distribution of literature. In absence of the president, the commander is in charge of the various classes and the overall spiritual atmosphere of the temple.

In addition, each temple has a treasurer and specially designated cooks. The worldwide ISKCON movement is divided into twelve administrative areas. The GBC (Governing Board Committee), a group of twelve area presidents, meets when necessary, although most of their work is handled by means of letters and memoranda. If for any reason a devotee disagrees with the decision made by his temple president, he may appeal it to his area's representative on the Governing Board Committee. Should a further appeal be made, it would go directly to Srila Prabhupada.

Daily Schedule

Monday through Friday the Philadelphia temple follows a regular schedule of activities:

3:30 A.M.	Devotees rise, shower, and dress
4:00 A.M.	Mangala-aratrika ("the most auspicious offering of the day")
4:30– 6:00 A.M.	Japa (chanting the Hare Krishna mantra sixteen rounds)
6:00 A.M.	Prayers to the spiritual master, Sri Bhagavatam
7:00 A.M.	Aratrika (breakfast offering)
7:45 A.M.	Nectar of Devotion class
8:15 A.M.	Prasadam (breakfast) and cleaning of temple
10:30 A.M.	Prasadam (lunch)
11:30– 4:45 P.M.	Sankirtana (public chanting of the Hare Krishna mantra on the city streets)
4:00 P.M.	Aratrika (evening offering)

5:30 P.M.	Prasadam (evening meal)
6:00 P.M.	Sri Isopanishad class
6:30 P.M.	*Bhagavad-Gita* class
7:00 P.M.	Aratrika (milk offering)
7:30 P.M.	Milk prasadam
8:30 P.M.	Reading of "the Krishna book" (*Krishna: The Supreme Personality of Godhead*)
9:00 P.M.	Free time for study
9:30 P.M.	Devotees retire

The daily schedule is flexible and is changed from time to time particularly at the smaller temples. The Philadelphia temple is so small that when a sankirtana party is late, the entire evening schedule must be delayed since the party consists of virtually all the Philadelphia devotees.

Rules

There are four main rules of conduct binding upon all devotees. I call them the "four don'ts": *No meat. No impure sex. No intoxicants. No gambling.* (1) The eating of meat, fish, and eggs, is prohibited. As one devotee put it, "You begin by eating flesh of animals, you continue by eating the flesh of other men, and you conclude by eating your own child." (2) Sexual relations are not allowed outside of marriage and are permitted only for the propagation of "Krishna Conscious children." (3) No intoxicants (not even tea and coffee) are allowed. Medicine may be taken if needed, but preparations containing narcotics are to be avoided whenever possible. (4) No gambling is allowed. This prohibition is extended to include "frivolous sports and games," interpreted by the spiritual master to mean conversation not concerned with

Krishna Consciousness. Hence, it is fruitless to try to engage the devotees in discussion of a point of view other than that of ISKCON. Despite the Hindu recognition of many paths to the Divine, the followers of Krishna have nothing but scorn for other religious movements. Many devotees have told me: "When you know the perfect way, why should you concern yourself with lesser ways? They are nothing but chaos and confusion anyhow."

The rules may appear simple. But they allow the sect to have complete mental and physical control over its members. As Daniel Cohen has written, "Devotees are not allowed to hold opinions other than those acceptable to Prabhupada and are, in fact, discouraged from thinking at all."[3] Marriages are arranged for single devotees, mates being recommended by the temple president. The individual has no idea when or whom he or she will marry. The belief that the unmarried state is unnatural is distinctively Hindu. After childhood and the student's life, the young person is expected to marry and live as a householder. After the birth of one's first grandchild, he may retire to the life of a forest dweller in order to seek spiritual liberation. But he cannot refuse the responsibilities of family life. There is no question that ISKCON's practice of taking young adults directly from school or incipient careers and transforming them into temple devotees is a distortion of Hindu norms as sanctified by the Vedic scriptures and as practiced in India. Prabhupada, it would seem, has created an order of almost totally ascetic priests and nuns more reminiscent of Buddhism and medieval Catholicism than Hinduism. Because of the preponderance of male devotees and the discouragement of family life in the temple, the householder stage commanded by Hindu tradition scarcely exists.

Women hold a distinctively inferior role in Krishna Consciousness—as they do in all the cults surveyed in this book. One wonders if the cults have not arisen as a response, in some measure, to the women's liberation movement and contemporary cultural confusion concerning sexual identity. Women's apparel holds far less spiritual significance. They are considered lacking in intelligence and are viewed as sources of confusion and temptation. Apart from the obligation to conceive children for the movement—couples may engage in sexual relations only once a month, at the time of greatest fertility—women have little place in the divine scheme as propounded by ISKCON. Small wonder that men outnumber women three to one in many temples.

Ordinarily all temple presidents are householders. When I visited the Philadelphia temple in 1971, two children lived there with their parents. Toys were at a minimum. I saw one doll and a few miscellaneous small items. The children were usually very quiet, with the three-year-old girl often joining in the chanting during the aratrika ceremonies. Since that time, a school was opened by the movement in Texas to which the children of devotees are sent for other "mundane" and "spiritual" instruction. However, failure to comply with state standards of instruction and the certification of teachers led to the closing of the school. The ISKCON conception of education has no place for science, history, or even English. Students are drilled in Hindu scriptures, obedience to sect rules, and Sanskrit.

Back to Godhead

In many ways, the lifeblood of ISKCON is the lavishly colored magazine *Back to Godhead.* The monthly publication not only proclaims the essential teachings of ISKCON to the uninitiated, but it is a major source of revenue for the movement. The contents are fairly stylized. The opening page contains a short statement of ISKCON philosophy and is usually decorated with a photograph of devotees chanting in some easily recognizable place, e.g., before the Colosseum in Rome. Page 2, titled "Chant and Be Happy—," consists of testimonies to the value of worshiping Krishna from followers who maintain secular employment as well as from temple devotees. Next is a full-page photograph of "His Divine Grace A. C. Bhaktivedanta Swami Prabhupada, Founder-Acarya of the International Society of Krishna Consciousness." There is usually a philosophical article comparing the teachings of a famous Western theologian, such as Thomas Aquinas, with Krishna Consciousness, to the extreme detriment of the former. One or two articles seemingly devoted to a topic of current interest follow. But after a paragraph, they become tedious expositions of Hindu scriptures.

Articles attacking modern science are frequent. The straw-man technique is prevalent. Science is reduced to an absurd generality; e.g., science is atheistic and concerned with creating life in test tubes. One is reminded of the sermons against evolution that were preached in Fundamentalist Christian churches for decades after the Scopes trial. Many pages are given to lengthy commentaries by Prabhupada on the Sanskrit text of some ancient scripture, interviews with Prabhupada, remarks in praise of Prabhupada, etc. There are news features—the most common topic being the ongoing struggle between ISKCON and parents of devotees bent on regaining their children through the courts or by recourse to deprogrammers.

Back to Godhead is excellent in the attainment of the goal it does not set out to reach and a poor vehicle for achieving the purpose for which it is chiefly used. As an instrument of evangelism, it is a bust. Its appeal is chiefly to the converted. Its technique of preaching to the potential convert ranges from assaultive and simplistic to muddled and obscure. If the reader already knows a great deal about Hinduism, he will be able to comprehend and perhaps appreciate the contents of *Back to Godhead*. Those unfamiliar with ISKCON will note the brightly colored, exotic pictures and be left wondering who these strange-looking people are and what they are doing. Millions of dollars are being spent on the dissemination of literature that might as well be mimeographed and distributed only in ISKCON temples, considering that its impact is limited principally to the temples. The magazine reiterates basic ISKCON doctrine, communicates the message of Prabhupada to his followers, reminds the devotees who ISKCON's enemies are (parents and scientists), and provides updates on movement projects (the opening of new temples, the development of agricultural projects, the publication of the ever-growing number of books by Prabhupada—approximately fifty of which have appeared to date). The image of Krishna Consciousness that *Back to Godhead* conveys is one of global growth and success together with hysterical defensiveness, opposition to the American way of life—especially materialism, self-indulgence, meat-eating, and attempts to maintain the integrity of the family against ISKCON efforts to win the children. Above all looms the countenance of a gnarled old holy man whose thoughts are the only thoughts expressed or tolerated.

A. C. Bhaktivedanta

And who is the elderly guru who exercises such control over the thoughts and behavior of hundreds of young Americans? For second only to the sheer ecstasy of chant-

Place of veneration of the spiritual master. ISKCON temple, Philadelphia.

Photo by Glen A. rierce.

ing is the devotion shown to the spiritual master, the founder of ISKCON, His Divine Grace A. C. Bhaktivedanta Swami Prabhupada. Krishna Consciousness was introduced to the United States by the then seventy-year-old swami in 1965. According to *Back to Godhead* magazine, the official periodical of ISKCON:

> Historically, the background of the Krishna consciousness movement can be traced back 5,000 years to the time when Lord Sri Krishna, the Supreme Personality of the Godhead, appeared on earth and explained to His personal friend Arjuna the philosophy of *Bhagavad-gita*. The practical application of the philosophical ideas of *Bhagavad-gita* was later clarified and simplified, 500 years ago, by Lord Sri Caitanya Mahaprabhu. . . . Lord Caitanya is understood from Vedic scriptural evidence to be an incarnation of God Himself who appeared on earth to teach the people of the modern age of quarrel and hypocrisy how to develop love of God. This Lord Caitanya did by introducing the *sankirtana* movement, or the congregational chanting of the holy name of God.

His Divine Grace A. C. Bhaktivedanta Swami Prabhupada

is the world teacher of the philosophy of Krishna consciousness as originally expounded by Lord Sri Krishna and propagated by Lord Caitanya Mahaprabhu. Speaking from the most elevated platform of complete God consciousness, Srila Prabhupada is offering us a simple, sure and direct method by which we can revive our dormant loving relationship with the Supreme Lord and thus attain perfection in this lifetime.

Srila Prabhupada came from India at the behest of *his* spiritual master, Bhaktisiddhanta Sarasvati, to preach the love of the Lord Krishna in the West. He is, says *Back to Godhead,*

> in a line of disciplic succession going back directly 500 years to the time when Lord Caitanya appeared in India (Lord Caitanya being considered Krishna himself in the role of a pure devotee), and from there back still further—5,000 years—to the time when the Lord Sri Krishna first spoke *Bhagavad-gita.*[4]

When the spiritual master arrived in New York in September of 1965 to undertake his mission, he rented a storefront in the East Village, a former souvenir shop named Matchless Gifts. According to Richard M. Levine: "Srila Prabhupada . . . just sat there in the middle of the floor in a lotus position, with mrdonga (drum) on his lap, and chanted. Among the local hippies, it soon became known as one of the better highs to turn on and go groove on the swami's music."[5] Many of the original visitors have become the movement's most fervent converts, and through them it has spread throughout the United States. If a devotee remains in the movement for a year or two, he will probably have the opportunity to meet His Divine Grace in person, since Srila Prabhupada travels about between the major temples. The following incident illustrates the sense of veneration felt for the spiritual master by the devotees. (Similar experiences have been recounted to me by followers of several prophet-founders.) Subinanda, twenty, has been a devotee for one and a half years and an initiate for one year. He relates "two sudden religious experiences." The first was in February of 1971 in St. Louis. He was reading in the back issues of *Back to Godhead* about an illness that had befallen the spiritual master necessitating his return to India for treatment. Subinanda notes:

> While reading this article I got filled with a tremendous sense of real love for my Spiritual Master—not a detached intellectual acceptance of my Spiritual Master, but actually a feeling of tremendous gratitude. And it became larger and larger—this feeling augmented and augmented—a feeling of dependence. . . . It began to dawn on me what my Spiritual Master was doing—what the actual relationship between my Spiritual Master and me was—that he actually was lifting me from ignorance. I had never had a religious inclination, and never thought in these kinds of terms—you know, darkness and light, and God, and anything like this. . . . I've changed since I've been in the movement. So, the only terms I could think of was this: that our Spiritual Master is bringing us from the darkness of ignorance to the light of knowledge—self-knowledge . . . and I got filled with the profundity of His Divine Grace A. C. Bhaktivedanta Swami Prabhupada.
> . . I was being filled with an immediate sense of the holiness of this individual, this man, A. C. Bhaktivedanta Swami Prabhupada. And the thoughts of him just filled my mind—it was almost like a trance state—I could think of nothing else. What I was thinking was: "It's too good to be true; it's too good to be true." I was thinking of all the craziness in the world—all the injustice . . . —all the rampant insanity on every level . . . and then I was thinking of my Spiritual Master, and that actually he was a saintly personality, and he was actually coming to deliver people from this, and I was being delivered from this.
> And this feeling became so strong that I began to cry. First

some tears—then bawling. I began to bawl like a child. I actually couldn't stop. And I was feeling a tremendous sense of purification. . . .

I had a tremendous sense of happiness—filled with happiness—a reservoir of happiness—just oozing out of every pore—just so nice. It didn't leave as suddenly as it came; it left me with a very profound sense of the sacredness of things—the holiness of things—everything is holy.

He recalls a similar feeling in somewhat different circumstances some time later. He was in Austin, Texas:

I was at the Hare Krishna temple there for a while, and it was at the airport—we were seeing off one of the devotees who was going for a few days' trip to Los Angeles. As we were seeing him off—he was a very, very nice devotee. . . . I've never been sentimental but I began to cry. Like here, feeling a sense of loss—this devotee was going for a few days to Los Angeles. And after a very short while this sense of love and separation was transferred to my Spiritual Master and I had the same kind of overwhelming feelings and profound veneration and love for my Spiritual Master as if he were right there inside of me. . . . I felt something very transcendental, as if I was tripping. I looked up at the sky and it was filled with colorations. My whole body and mind was filled with happiness.

And I thought, "How wonderful that I feel so happy. I never thought I could feel this happy!" And that thought would be impetus for a much greater feeling of happiness, and I became progressively more and more happy until I was almost bursting. And I did—I started crying. I didn't want to—I was embarrassed—it was a public place. I wasn't pure and able to express myself in that way—I was a little bit inhibited about that. So I was actually trying to erase all these nice thoughts from my mind—to bring myself down, but I really couldn't—and it felt so good! Again, it was a feeling of purification.

And the actual pattern of my thought was like this: "It's too good to be true—it's too good to be true—that Srila Prabhupada exists. Considering the hellish condition of the world; that there is one solid thing to hold on to. Here's one person who is actually fully sane, and in addition to being fully sane, he has the power to transmit transcendental knowledge to others—this was all too good to be true. I was reflecting over my entire past life and realizing now that everything was becoming good—everything was heading in a positive direction. By becoming a disciple of this man I was in a progressive march upwards toward realization, towards freedom. . . .

In both of these incidents I was filled with a sense of perfection— that there was some perfection, and that I was moving towards it. And at the same time I was thinking of Prabhupada, I was also thinking about Krishna.

Think about Prabhudpada. Think about Krishna. Think about nothing else. For the devotees of ISKCON, that is the key. But can they—or should they—"stay high forever"? As anyone who has encountered the Hare Krishnas will attest, the ISKCON life-style is bizarre and strange. Moreover, the values by which these young neo-Hindus have come to live, the understanding of reality upon which their daily actions are based, has produced in them a perception of the so-called normal world by virtue of which it is we who seem bizarre and strange to them. A "normal" observer such as myself finds them colorful, unusual, and, in many ways, charming. At the same time, I consider them totally absorbed in a romanticized and unrealistic philosophy that deprives them of opportunities for personal development or effectual impact upon our society. The more they become lost in their own imagery, the more difficult does it become for them to communicate with us or for us to reach them. This group, the most visible of all new religious cults in America, shows the least prospect of integrating itself into the tapestry of our communal expectations or the fabric of our lives.

V. IS ALL THIS REALLY NECESSARY?

Cults are highly unpopular with the overwhelming majority of the adults with whom I converse on a day-to-day basis. Many of my acquaintances will not discuss cults. The slightest reference to the Moonies, for example, evokes expressions of dread, frustration, and hostility. "Is all this nonsense really necessary?" I am frequently asked.

Parents have always been beset by the fear that their children would not live up to those aspirations and expectations in which they as parents have invested so much. As sociologist Robin M. Williams, Jr., has remarked, our culture is marked "by a central stress upon personal achievement, especially secular occupation achievement. The 'success story' and the respect accorded to the self-made man are distinctly American. Did not

William James chide us a half century ago for our national disease, the worship of the bitch-goddess SUCCESS"?[1] Above all, we want our children to succeed. We want them to get ahead, to move up the economic ladder, to be respected. Nothing could be more threatening to our vision of what we want our children to want for themselves than the message of the cults. For, on the surface at least, the cults say abandon all secular and materialistic aspirations, ignore what the world thinks of you, welcome persecution and self-sacrifice.

Parent after parent has said to me: "I don't understand. I just don't understand. What's wrong with these young people? They haven't even lived long enough to know what they are giving up. If only I had had the opportunities that they have." Having a son or daughter reject our aspirations, values, and way of life is a disappointing and disorienting experience. But it is also an experience that forces us to question our assumptions of what we want for our children. For the basic question should be: *What do our children want for themselves?*

Having spent much of three decades on college campuses, I have seen several approaches to this question. To generalize, young adults of the 1950s wanted to fit in, to adjust, to be accepted, to succeed. For them a college education was a passport to a good-paying job, a house in the suburbs, and the respect of one's neighbors. The college student of the fifties could conform to the standards imposed upon him by society because he could accept the viability of that society. And there was ample room for him in that society—unless he was black or a beatnik or a communist. The student of the sixties would not commit himself to the cozy assumptions of the previous generation. The sixties brought a generation of noisy dissidents bent upon avoiding the unquestioning conformity of the student of the fifties. Every generation of young adults has questioned the values of their elders, but the college students of the sixties were more than critics of the status quo. For the Vietnamese war provided a focus for minor social revolutions. And energies that previously had fueled only the acceptable, harmless pranks of youth now were directed against the established order. Vietnam not only divided this nation but encouraged every dissenter whatever his or *her* cause to challenge the system that had tolerated and countenanced the moral muddle of American foreign policy. Conflict over the war in Asia created a climate of assault upon every social convention.

Traditional sexual morality was attacked as repressive. Accustomed sexual roles were seen as inequitable and exploitative. Prohibitions on the use of such substances as marijuana and LSD were flaunted (sometimes with reasoned appeals, more often with utter disregard for the need to reason at all). Still there was ample room in the economy, and, somehow, each side was able to accommodate the other. And besides, the rebels were never more than a minority—a highly visible, discordant, and all too influential minority in the eyes of the media perhaps, but a minority nonetheless.

The present college generation lives with a realization that sets them apart from those who have gone before them. *There is no longer ample room.* At least half those who received a college education in the seventies will experience the spirit-crushing humiliation of finding themselves a surplus commodity. Education no longer guarantees upward mobility. It does not even guarantee a job. The vast majority of recent college graduates are employed in positions that short years ago were the domain of those without college degrees. According to the United States Department of Labor, by the time this book is published all professions—including medicine—may well be stocked to the brim.[2] The students in my classes in the early sixties were fascinating. They were experimenters, advocates, adversaries, and idealists. The students of the late sixties were frustrating. They expected immediate gratification of every need, instant redress for every grievance (real or imagined), the maximum return for the least possible effort. But my dealings with the college students of the seventies conjures up one mood more than any other—*depression.*

They were depressed, and as a teacher I was often depressed by the lack of enthusiasm, unwillingness to work, and decreased abilities of my students. By 1970, the basic student skills of reading, writing, and computation could no longer be presupposed. Grades had been devalued during the Vietnamese war when academic failure could cancel a student's draft deferment. Entrance standards were down in the name of greater opportunity for disadvantaged youths. Hard work and discipline were passé. And word was getting around that there were few jobs. Glum prospects produced withdrawn, despondent students who received little public attention. "Insecurity," notes Joel Kotkin, "has produced a deep, internalized despair among young people. Such numbing emotions are not likely to be picked up by the news media because pervasive depression is not usually very expressive." [3]

In some ways, the campuses seem to have come back to the mood of the fifties. The word is: "Stay cool. Don't get involved. Don't mess up; you are going to have a hard enough time getting a job." But the student of the fifties was willing to play by the rules of middle America. The student of the seventies finds those rules unworkable. The rejection of middle-class standards of behavior that characterized the rebels of a few years ago is still a fixture of the youth culture. But the vision of anything resembling an alternative life-style has not yet emerged. Most young people want the security of middle-class existence, but they have none of the attitudes, values, or standards upon which such a way of life is based. In the words of one critic, "Today's young people . . . are bereft of either the passions and causes of the '60's or the self-discipline and internal restraints built into young Americans of earlier generations." [4]

Lack of restraint and career-orientation are a poor mix. In the eyes of today's young adult (and many of his elders), traditional sources of leadership and authority cannot be trusted. But no new ones have come along to take their place. It is a difficult time to come to adulthood. It is an equally difficult time to be an adult. At no time since the Great Depression have the pre-adult years been so excruciatingly painful. No longer children and not yet adults, young people must endure confusion and anxiety. Dissatisfied with their state and powerless to change it, they direct their frustrated anger at their parents and all adult-controlled institutions. Some try to change the society against which they harbor such resentment. Others stubbornly hang on, expressing their disenchantment with abundant cynicism. A few reject that society as beyond redemption, choosing to drop out and seek some private salvation through drugs, violence, oriental philosophy, or life in a rural commune. Some adopt what psychiatrist Erik Erikson terms "a negative identity," rejecting everything that their parents taught them to value and valuing everything their parents taught them to reject. Most flow from one immediate satisfaction to the next with no fixed direction or goal. *And many become converts!*

Why does an individual join a cult? To escape self-dissatisfaction, loneliness, and boredom. When is an individual most susceptible to the lure of a religious movement? When he is unhappy with himself; when the demands upon him seem too great and his resouces too meager; when the future seems murky, and all that appears ahead in the tunnel is more tunnel.

What leads one toward religious conversion? In the past, individuals and societies have been most susceptible to religious experience during periods of scarcity, uncertainty, hopelessness, and boredom. When there is great want and frustration, men and women will turn to powers greater than themselves for aid and comfort. When established values break down and the future appears threatening, they will likewise *turn away* from all that they associate with suffering and anxiety and turn *toward* anyone or anything that seems to offer a way of escape.

The young adults whose conversion experiences I have studied knew little of deprivation. They were well housed, well fed, well clothed by their elders. It was not a sense of material insecurity that led them to seek beyond the mundane world. They suffered a terrible emptiness—a lack not of the necessities of life but of the values that make life human, humane, and fulfilling. Above all, they were motivated to seek personal salvation by an overwhelming sense of ennui. It may well be the case that no society has ever enjoyed a higher general level of freedom from want or a more pervasive sense of boredom and loneliness. After all, when life is an endless struggle for survival no one is ever bored. When men and women are united in a life-and-death conflict as they were during the Second World War, who is lonely?

Is their need real or neurotic? Are the satisfactions they seek essential or illusory? Are they saints or spoiled brats? Prophets of a better way, or self-indulgent dilettantes? Do they provide alternative life-styles or temporary entertainment? Even if we cannot accept them at face value, we owe them more than our skeptical, out-of-hand rejection. Can we really offer them a more engaging, challenging, and fulfilling way of life than the alternatives provided by the cults?

Religious Conversion

Religious conversion is scarcely the invention of current cults. Writing at the beginning of the present century, William James reported:

> To be converted, to be regenerated, to receive grace, to experience religion, to gain an assurance, are so many phrases which denote the progress, gradual or sudden by which a self hitherto divided, and consciously wrong, inferior, and unhappy, becomes unified and consciously right, superior, and happy, in consequence of its firmer hold upon religious realities.[5]

Although religious conversion is *apparently* sudden at its onset, it is often the result of a long process through which the divided self has dealt with religious realities. The event of conversion is unexpected and seemingly spontaneous. Yet the process of incubation may have been gradual and lengthy.

Some observers feel that conversion is *progressive* and regenerative, resulting in definite personality development. Others feel that conversion is essentially *regressive*, encouraging childlike dependence and stunting personal growth. Leon Salzman feels that many conversion experiences lead only to a "pseudo-solution: of the problem of personal failure and guilt." [6]

On the one hand, conversion can create an exaggerated intensity of belief, intolerance toward those whose interpretation of this belief differs from that of the convert, an overzealous drive to convert others, and a masochistic need for martyrdom and self-punishment.[7] On the other, it can provide one with a center, a sense of meaning and identity, a faith that integrates all of one's experiences. Whether we view religious conversion as essentially progressive or regressive, it should be recognized that the conversion experience can produce a loss of orientation, a sense of disintegration, and alienation. Obviously, the adjectives one chooses to describe a conversion experience—whether it is one's own experience or that of another—reflect the value judgments that one has made concerning such experiences. What one person considers an experience that provides meaning to life, a second person may regard as a childish and irrational act.

Is there a personality type that is more prone to religious conversion than are others? William James spoke of a "self-surrender type" of individual, one who is especially suggestible and more likely to lose his equilibrium and be reduced to a sense of inadequacy.[8] Psychiatrist John P. Kildahl describes those susceptible to conversion as generally less intelligent and more hysterical than other comparable individuals. The prospective convert, he maintains, is "subject to mood swings, excitability, fearfulness." In such a personality, "naivete and moralism are particularly evident: as is a 'general tendency toward over-responsiveness to the emotional implication of events to the exclusion of (the) rational.' "[9] My own investigations have found converts to be of generally superior intelligence although somewhat emotionally and sexually immature.

Nearly twenty years ago, D. A. Windermuller compared the religious conversions experienced during the eighteenth-century evangelical revival with the "brainwashing" techniques employed by the Chinese communists. He concludes that both phenomena have much in common in that (1) they are crisis experiences and problem-solving processes that aid in maintaining ego identity and in creating a state of inner harmony; (2) they involve emotional upheaval that produces changes in an individual's thinking and behavior; (3) they depend on group pressures involving interrogation, confession, and discussion; (4) they rely on highly structured organizations; (5) they introduce new vocabulary; (6) they use exhaustion and suggestion; (7) they produce self-criticism, doubt, fear, and guilt; (8) they offer feelings of cleanness, light, relief; and (9) they repress one aspect of the individual's psychic system and the coming to conscious control of another.[10] I would conclude from these interesting parallels that conversion is an experience that is neither wholly good nor wholly evil. Some will be threatened by such a comparison. Conversion, they will assert, is "the operation of the Holy Spirit" and is thus "forever beyond the powers of human observation." But the fact that such experiences occur in contexts other than that of Christian revivalism (e.g., a Billy Graham crusade) and that they can involve conceptual objects other than the revivalist's God would suggest that conversion is not restricted to any given tradition. It would seem that personality factors are primary, and the ideological content secondary. Whether it is a tent meeting, a marathon encounter group, a drug-induced "mystical" state, "coming clean" through Scientology, or a myriad of other conversion experiences—the one constant seems to be the placing of the conversion-prone psyche in the midst of a crisis-causing group rather than a set of teachings. As my hippie friends told me years ago, "When you trip, setting is everything."

Another fundamental truth of the nature of conversion experiences is that they are seldom as radical as they appear. Very few of the religious converts whom I have interviewed were from nonreligious backgrounds. Only an estimated one in ten describes himself as having been an "atheist" or "without religious background" prior to conversion. Most converts report that they had become disenchanted with or indifferent to their childhood religion. But seldom does the convert move directly from no relationship to religion to total religious commitment. The most common form of conversion is not a change in religious affiliation but a change in attitude toward the religion of one's youth.[11] Religious experience is not the establishment of contact with hitherto unknown sacred power as much as it is the transformation of the quality of this contact.

The message seems clear, those who from childhood have participated in religious rituals in the home as well as at places of worship have a starting point for their religious quests. If the attitudes of awe, devotion, and concern for others are obvious in the behavior of family members and friends, it is likely that such attitudes will be recreated in the lives of the next generation. If one's family is only nominally religious or the quality of their participation in religious ritual suggests attendance at a theater rather than membership in a community united by the worship of God and the fellowship of brethren, it is unlikely that a young adult will interpret his later religious experiences within his parents' sphere of understanding.

A few more observations concerning the background of converts are in order. Those young adults who feel that the religion of their parents is grim, repressive, and compulsive will undoubtedly rebel against it. They may pass through a period of "negative formation," a time in which all the prohibitions of the past are violated. But such violation frequently proves as obsessive as the attitudes against which they protest. There are tremendous stress, dread, and anxiety in the breaking of taboos. Some of the most dedicated disciples of religious cults and a disproportionate share of cult leadership are drawn from the ranks of those who stand in rebellion against a highly structured, morally demanding religious upbringing. Strict conformity—even when it is forced upon the individual—is seldom replaced by lethargy. The children of moral, religious zealots often become moral, religious zealots. But the convert's morality and religion and those of his parents may be poles apart. The son of a tent evangelist may become an archbishop of the Children of God.

But what of the children of religiously neutral and ethically permissive parents? Are they immune to the appeal of the cults? Certainly not. For every child of strict, conservative parents who finds his or her way into an authoritarian cult, there are at least ten children from liberal, tolerant families. The child of parents with clear commitments has something against which to react, attitudes to reject or refine, and a haven to which he may return if all else fails. "Live and let live" provides no sense of direction. How can anyone find a fixed point of reference in a stress-filled world by reacting to such an attitude as that reflected in the often-heard parental cop-out: "I don't believe in forcing my children to do anything they don't want to. I think they should have the right to think for themselves, to decide on their own values and beliefs. I think that when they are adults they can choose their own religion." If only parents who feel this way would realize that they are telling their children: "I really don't care what you believe or how you choose to behave as long as you don't hurt yourself or embarass me. I just make out the best I can from day to day. I don't know what I believe; so how can I encourage you to follow in my steps?" How much better it would be if we admitted our own lack of faith to our children instead of patting ourselves on the back for our superiority to those who compel their children to conform to parental standards of faith and practice.

Thus far we have been emphasizing the convert and his conversion experience rather than the progressive restructuring of the individual's total life within the newfound community of fellow believers. We have seen that rootlessness, insecurity, and lack of hope set the stage for conversion. And we have noted some of the consequences of conversion in terms of transformation of the life of individuals. Conversion experiences may occur in a variety of settings. However, what the cults provide that many other conversion experiences lack is a total pattern for the expression of heightened emotions. For unless intense experiences are articulated and routinized in accordance with some established norms, they quickly fade away. When newly discovered religious energies are channeled according to the teachings and ethical standards of a community of faith, they may become the basis for a total transformation of the individual's personality and way of life.

In general, there is a ratio between the demands that the community makes upon the individual and the degree of personal transformation that is possible. In other words, the more total and involving the commitment of the individual, the greater will be the personal satisfaction the convert finds. Unfortunately, as the degree of commitment and satisfaction increases, so does the possibility of delusion and harm. The cults we have examined in these pages are examples of "total trips." The Children of God, the disciples of the Unification Church, and the devotees of Krishna provide fascinating illustrations of religious communities that offer a totally structured, religiously oriented alternative way of life.

In each cult, there is a daily routine that encompasses every thought, feeling, and act. From the moment the convert wakes in the morning until he retires at night, every ounce of energy is directed toward the goals of the group. There is no privacy, no contact with critics or dissenters, no opportunity for reflection. No group member is allowed to travel unaccompanied by other members. Worship, work, play, even marriage and procreation of children are strictly controlled by the movement. The members of these cults speak little other than quotations from the teachings of the founder of the movement.

As I left the warehouse headquarters of the Children of

God, two things caught my eye. The first was the happy homogeneity of the disciples. Like the members of all the cults I have studied, the Children were almost uniform. The personal idiosyncratic tendencies that made one convert different from another and of interest as a separate human being were to them matters of regret. How often a COGer or a Hare Krishna has caught himself being himself and has *apologized* to me. The other thing to which my attention was riveted at COG headquarters was a sign in the kitchen: There Is No Room for Self Here.

A total trip. A simple transaction: total fulfillment in return for total subjection.

I spoke not long ago at a suburban congregation of the United Church of Christ on the appeal of contemporary religious sects. Parents whose children are approaching adulthood were quite concerned. "How can our church be as attractive to our young people as the religious groups you have described?" I was asked. "You can't compete," I responded, "unless you are willing to be as demanding as the cults. Are you willing to ask young people to give up comfort, security, and pleasure in order to devote their whole lives to your faith? Do you have a vision of a better world that they can actualize *now* through the full-time devotion of their every thought, word, and deed? If not, you cannot win." Neither the minister nor the congregation liked what I had to say. For I was generating images of the kind of religion many of them had experienced as children—authoritarian, moralistic, intolerant. They did not want their children to suffer. And that's the point. Many of their children do.

For them, the cults are coming.

VI. GROUP LEADERS, GREED, AND COERCION

"I know the truth will set me free. The question is, How much will it set me back?" So begins an advertisement for the Expanding Circle, which for an annual fee provides discounts at seminars, workshops, consultations, etc., offered by organizations ranging from the Aquarian Age Yoga Centre in Virginia Beach, Virginia, to the Wholistic Health and Nutrition Institute in Mill Valley, California.

The cults flourishing in our midst promise the individual total fulfillment in exchange for complete obedience. But what do they really cost? How much will they set us back?

The first criticism made of an emerging religious sect in America has to do with its finances. Our society, which so idolizes monetary success in other spheres, applies a strange standard to spiritual movements: Poverty and purity are somehow regarded as identical. At least critics of religion are fair. They are as likely to fault the Roman Catholic Church for its conspicuous collection of art treasures and real estate as they are to count the number of Cadillacs owned by a self-proclaimed messiah. The adherents of cults are models of sacrificial asceticism. They not only give up everything to follow their faith—give it up *to* the group—but their lives are given in large measure to raising funds for the cult. They are clearly not in it for the money.

The prophet-founder of any given cult is another matter. The gurus and the institutions they have founded flaunt spectacular wealth. Maharaj Ji lives like a maharajah. Before Sun Myung Moon visits a local Unification Church his followers have been known to raise enormous sums through candle sales to purchase a suitable domicile for him. While his followers slave twelve hours a day to raise money for the church, he lives like a Greek shipping magnate. Thousands of Children of God, most of them destitute but many of them of means, have surrendered all to Moses David. While he languishes in luxury, they support themselves and the movement through the sale of COG literature and artifacts. The opulence that surrounds A. C. Bhaktivedanta Swami Prabhupada delights the heart of his every disciple.

In almost every case, the properties, vehicles, publishing houses, and factories of the cult belong not to the leader but to the movement. What glorifies him brings honor to them. The whole world belongs to God, Christ, or Krishna, they reason. Why should the Landlord of Creation desire squalor for those chosen by him? Disciples feel neither despoiled nor exploited. Because the leader asks nothing for himself and offers total fulfillment, no gift is too great for him. I have seen followers of a given cult compete with one another to solicit the most for the leader on a crowded street corner. On occasion, I have encountered the followers of two or more different groups at the same location pursuing tourists for contributions. I have overheard these collectors of loose dollars returning to their place of domicile, flushed with the victory of goals surpassed.

A devotee of Krishna with a street party was entering the Sri Sri Radha Krishna Temple in Berkeley with a street party as my wife and I were departing. He said to us: "When I was a child I used to hear about heaven—a place of beautiful sights, sounds, and odors; with wonderful food in abundance; and many friends. I have that now— here in the temple." I have seen this particular devotee wearing a Continental soldier's costume, selling flowers and *Back to Godhead* magazine at Fisherman's Wharf in San Francisco. He and his party wear such disguises to conceal their exotic Hindu appearance. White wigs and three-cornered hats conceal their shaven heads. Their Revolutionary War garb causes curiosity and leads to conversation, whereas their temple attire evokes fear and disdain. I have watched him and his partners skillfully work the tourists for two- and three-dollar donations "for students" or "for libraries" or "to help former drug addicts" or "to buy books for needy students." They are as effective as any of the street peddlers who crowd the area. I have watched this particular devotee gleefully counting out the money in his pocket. It delights him that he is able to acquire so much for Krishna.

This devotee has neither been hypnotized nor kidnapped. If he were selling handcrafted leather goods or copper bracelets, he would, considering his skill as a salesman, be able to sustain himself quite adequately. His conversation is shallow, revealing a one-track mind. From my point of view, he is annoyingly immature. But no one is holding him againt his will. He is free to leave the Sri Sri Radha Krishna Temple at any time. As I left him one day after a conversation that cost me two dollars in contributions to ISKCON, I passed a T-shirt shop that displayed several hundred designs available for instant application. One read as follows: I Have Abandoned My Search for Truth and Am Now Looking for a Good Fantasy.

Part of the good fantasy, or "truth," of each of the cults is the virtual worship of the founder-prophet. Yet I cannot say that I find any of the current cult leaders to be particularly attractive heroes. None of them elicits the adulation that I felt in my twenties when I heard John F. Kennedy address an outdoor audience in Philadelphia during his presidential campaign. Since the death of JFK, I have met more than a score of gurus, prophets, sect leaders, holy men, and theologians. I have known an assortment of media personalities, writers, philosophers, artists, and public officials, including a U.S. senator on whose national campaign staff I served. I understand what it is like to want to believe in someone, to seek in another human being a guide toward a hopeful future. I wish that I could find a commitment as total and a reward as full as those experienced by the followers of Sun Myung Moon et al. I admire the singleness of their purpose and the simplicity of their lives. But I have *not* abandoned my search for the truth, and I can allow only God to be God. Hence, I cannot stop questioning the claims of these new divinities.

Through the mass media our culture creates new deities by the hundreds. We regard them with awe. We shower them with adulation. We grant them power and majesty.

We consider their deaths cosmic events. How insignificant the immediate response to the death of Jesus seems when compared to the worldwide communion of grief that attended the assassination of President Kennedy or the shock of disbelief with which America shuddered when Elvis Presley died all too young amidst the tokens of success and glorification. Our hard-nosed, cynical secularism may have little room for God, but it lavishes its treasure and attention upon many deities. So why not Moses David, Moon, Prabhupada, and the rest?

Let us remember Subinda's moment of grief as a fellow devotee was about to depart. Notice once more the ingredients of his experience: his profound sense of loss, the refusal to direct this loss to its "true object," and the redirection of the feelings of the moment toward a "purely conceptual object"—the spiritual master. Finally, note the extent to which the empiric data have been reinterpreted in recollection with the passage of time. Was this conceptualization about A. C. Bhaktivedanta present in the mind of the devotee as he stood in the Austin airport? I doubt it.

What is going on in the minds of those who would worship a cult leader? They have been exposed to some personal trauma that has thrown them out of balance emotionally. They have sublimated their instinctual feelings. They have chosen to deal with a projected image in the form of the founder-prophet rather than the real cause of the upheaval. The redirection of their feelings has resulted in a sense of intense relief, release, and purification, in consequence of which they have found their senses stimulated and the mundane world transfigured. People who fall in love, who are born again, who turn on through the use of psychedelic drugs, who achieve a breakthrough in an encounter group, or who come clear through Scientology report experiences identical in structure.

The pattern of response to the object of these forms of experience is similar. The object of each form of experience (God, the Beloved, and the Leader, etc.) is both *numinous* and *charismatic*. According to Rudolf Otto's classic description, the holy, or numinous, is "wholly other." It is "quite beyond the sphere of the usual, the intelligible, and the familiar." It is a "living force," an almost electric energy that fills the individual by whom it is experienced with both fascination and dread. A tension is created that can never be resolved. The individual is attracted to a communion that transforms his life. At the same time, he is overpowered with a sense of obligation and unworthiness.[1] In the Judeo-Christian heritage, of course, such experiences pertain to God alone.

The intensity of the experience and the totality of the demands made by the object of the experience are inseparable. As Joachim Wach observes, religious experience is a "total response of the total being to what is apprehended as ultimate reality . . . the most intense experience of which man is capable."[2] But is not everything we have said about religious experience also true of the experiences of romantic love and commitment to a mass movement? Is not the first meeting of the lover and the beloved filled with awe—terror mingled with fascination? Does not the leader of the mass movement or the very concept upon which such a movement is based strike the individual with a sense of reverence—a feeling of unworthiness combined with a deep sense of obligation.

Further, is not the numinous indistinguishable from the charismatic? Despite the abuse of the word *charisma* in recent years, it is an extremely valuable concept for the understanding of religious experience and its substitutes. Max Weber defines charisma as

> a certain quality of an individual personality by virtue of which he is set apart from ordinary men and treated as endowed with supernatural, superhuman, or at least specifically exceptional powers of qualities. These are such as are not accessible to the ordinary person, but are regarded as of divine origin, or as exemplary. And on the basis of them the individual concerned is treated as a leader.[3]

Clearly charisma is the possession by an individual of "numinosity" or "wholly otherness." By virtue of charisma, the individual becomes an object of religious experience, romantic love, or the center of a new social reality. Does the object of devotion really possess "exceptional powers or qualities"? Or does charisma exist chiefly in the eye of the beholder? Clearly it is a meeting of both objective characteristics and subjective needs. The more intensely dissatisfied the individual is, the more he will project upon the mysterious other (be it person, deity, or movement) those qualities he finds most lacking in himself. But there must be something about the object that allows it to be the basis of such projection.

Much faith, of course, is blind faith that expects of its object what its object can never provide. For the more ignorant we are of our beloved, our leader, or our God at the time we make the brave and dangerous leap of self-commitment, the more we are able to suppress doubt and receive self-fulfillment in return for self-surrender. It is my personal opinion that there are few charismatic leaders in America. It is my experience that the incessant glare of the mass media soon dissipates the mystery and exposes the mundane humanity of all objects of devotion, thereby destroying the remote otherness upon which projection depends. Today's journalists—both print and electronic—have become increasingly cynical. They are not content until the last vestige of superiority has been stripped from every hero. Facts are construed in the most negative manner possible. Rumor is treated as fact; wild speculation as rational possibility. Through incessant representation and misrepresentation, heroes are ruthlessly cut down to size. Such practices may ensure that we will not soon place our trust in those who are not worthy of it. However, the present mood makes it difficult for us to accept any source of authority—political, educational, or religious.

A completely different logic is at work among the cults. It makes no difference what the facts are. The need to believe is so great for the cultist that he will ignore all that tends to discredit the founder-prophet. Media attention to Sun Myung Moon, for instance, has been overwhelmingly hostile. He is depicted as a tool of the South Korean government, a present-day Hitler, a discredited heretic who was excommunicated by his own church, a rip-off artist who has reaped millions from his underfed and overworked members. Such attacks are well known among the Moonies. If Moon were tomorrow convicted of stock manipulation or Mann Act violations and sentenced to prison, the hard core of his followers would simply dismiss the reality of the situation as Satan's attack upon God's chosen messenger. The cultist is desperate for structure, order, and authority. He or she cannot survive emotionally without them. Apart from the identity and support of the group, the life of the individual is lonely and trivial. A cultist is one who cannot *not* believe. Above all, the cultist needs to believe in belief itself. In this respect, the cultist is incredibly American. For ours is a society that believes not so much in God as in believing. Religion is regarded as a magic balm that instills moral values, dispels fear and guilt, creates confidence, mitigates our animal bloodlust, produces financial success, reduces tension, enables us to tolerate the intolerable, etc. Religion is the secret ingredient that mends broken hearts, rears perfect children, liberates from anxiety, comforts the afflicted, and afflicts the comfortable. *The whole nation is a sect that believes in religion even though the vast majority of us have only the most fleeting acquaintance with the doctrines or ritual practices of any specific religion.*

Why then do we find the cults so intolerable? Because they threaten to take our children away from us, from our values, from our aspirations. They seek to wrest our sons and daughters from all that is familiar and acceptable to us, all that makes us familiar and acceptable to others. In the minds of many parents, the cults have replaced drugs as the number one threat to our high school– and college-aged offspring.

VII. WHAT CAN WE DO?

The cults are coming. What charm can we hang on our doors to hold them at bay? How can we defend our families? How can we regain those dear to us who have already heard the siren call of the Unification Church, Krishna, or COG?

First, we must understand why the cults are so attractive to the young at this time in our nation's history. Enough has been said of such matters throughout this account of the cults.

Second, we must risk open communication with our children no matter how bare we strip our souls in the process. Pretending that there are no problems in our lives, no doubts, no failings, can only widen the gap between the generations. For who can honestly voice fears, admit shortcomings, and seek guidance in the presence of those who "are without sin"?

Third, we must recognize that what we cannot do for our children in the first eighteen or twenty years of their lives we are unlikely to accomplish by intervening when they become adults. This means two things: (a) The formative years must be taken seriously; and (b) the right of our children to make their own mistakes must be respected. From our children's birth to their late teens, we have the opportunity to convey our attitudes to the young, communicate our cherished beliefs, expose our familial and cultural heritage. By the time our children begin attending senior high school, most of them have spent between ten thousand and fifteen thousand hours watching television. We constantly decry the influence of television, its appeal to the mass mentality, its fixation with violence, its distortion of our values. Yet every television set has an off button. Your child may resist your suggestions that he or she do what you value, but a child seldom does anything as an alternative to television that is not in response to a parental example. Attitudes, the proverb goes, are caught; they are not taught.

Character-building is a term of a bygone age. Adults want everyone but themselves to accept responsibility for the transformation of children into adults. Have you ever taken your child to a national monument such as Valley Forge or the Battleship Arizona and explained what this special place means to you? Have you read a favorite poem aloud? Have you sat your child before your parents or grandparents and encouraged the elders to communiate family history and religious tradition? Have you explained what you believe about God, sex, money, and death—those awkward areas of human concern that adults hide from one another as well as from their children? Have you taken the time to explain what the struggle for adulthood was like for you so that your child will have some notion of what it will be like to come of age in a world like yours in many respects yet alien in others?

Children who are lost to their families after their conversion to a religious cult were probably lost to them before their conversion. "Johnny was such a loving son before he became a Hare Krishna," a distraught mother reports. Does she mean *loving* or *conforming*? Children who could openly discuss matters of importance in their lives with their parents before they were attracted to a religious sect usually will be able to keep the lines of communication open thereafter. Threatening the convert, maligning his or her religion, demanding conformance to your standards and values, will only produce a firmer resolve on the part of the convert to perservere in the path that has been chosen.

I pity those who resort to physical force and mental duress as means to restore their adult children to themselves. I am not insensitive to parental concern over children who are heedlessly harming their health, fortune, and prospects for the future. But I cannot condone coercion. When left to themselves, about three-quarters of all cult converts will become disenchanted within a very short time, frequently under ninety days. The surest way to produce a long-term fanatic is to persecute the new convert. Like all strong emotions, enthusiasm cannot be sustained indefinitely. Sometime during the first year a period of doubt and confusion ensues. Should well-meaning parents attempt to dissuade the convert, they will inadvertently add weight to the credibility of the cult. "We warned you that there would be persecution. The animosity of your family proves that you are a true child of God and that they are children of the devil." The confused young convert has a natural need to resist parental interference in general. He or she resents parental mandates on how to dress or who to date or what career to pursue even without the added probem of finding a satisfying religious identity. If parental meddling succeeds and the convert does leave the cult, what follows can be a return to childlike dependence upon parents and authority figures approved by parents. The former convert will lack confidence, be unable to make decisions, and suffer a serious loss of personal direction.

And should the effort to free the young adult from the clutches of the cult prove unsuccessful, everyone loses. Trust between child and parents is shattered. The halfhearted convert is transformed into the fully committed "true believer." For compromise would mean that one's parents have been right all along and the convert has been wrong. In either case—whether parents shake the foundations of their offspring's faith or not—seeds have been planted that sooner or later will yield a harvest of resentment. Love your child enough to cut the cord. Unless the issue is life or death, parents must be prepared to allow their adult progeny to make their own mistakes. The sole exception and one which conscience requires that we observe is the adult who is so physically or mentally ill that he or she is, in the eyes of the law, unable to provide for basic human needs of food, clothing, and shelter. Clearly, our society recognizes that parents or social agencies would be remiss if they did not intervene. In such cases, however, parents should seek competent professional guidance before taking rash action.

Sincerely motivated parents have made dreadful mistakes. But the record of the cults is far from perfect. I admire dedication, self-sacrifice, moral standards, and devotion to the actualization of ideals. However, there is much about the present religious cult scene that I personally abhor. First, religious groups ranging from traditional evangelistic to far-out sectarian have a tendency to justify unethical and dishonest practices. Too much convert-seeking is covert. People have a right to know the true name of the product that is being sold to them. Just as it is unfair to mislabel a patented medicine or food product, so it is wrong to present the gospel as "entertainment for the whole family," or the doctrines of the Unification Church as "experimentation with alternative family life-styles." I am incensed when a G-rated movie at the local theater turns out to be an evangelistic rally complete with preachers and altar calls. It is wrong to prosyletize young children without their parents' permission. Of course, the Bible is filled with prooftexts that can be cited. Sneaky evangelism is still morally repugnant. Likewise, it galls me when the cults conceal their true identities until they have removed the prospective convert from familiar surroundings and family influences.

Nor can I accept the deceptive manner in which the cults raise money. The purpose for which funds will be spent should be clearly identified when they are solicited. I am impressed by the salesmanship of the Moonies and the Hare Krishnas. But is the money really for "drug programs" or "welfare work among the poor" or "education" or "scholarships for needy students"? Again, it is easy to rationalize. Is it my fault, says the cultist, that what my faith means by education or welfare is different from what the donor understands by such terms? And with all the negative coverage we receive in the satanically controlled press, how much money do you think we would be able to raise for God's work if we revealed our true identity? As much as you deserve, I would reply. The dishonest zealot is a disgrace to his faith—whatever that faith may be.

There is a basic rule I try to apply to myself whenever I am convinced that I know what is best for another human being or a group of human beings. At such times, I always call to mind the following observation: *More harm has been done to mankind by unredeemed redeemers than by all the legions of hell.* To the prospective cultist and the current disciple, I would offer this advice: Ask now: Who is leading my parade? Where am I going. What is the real cost? Those who would deflect, divert, or coerce any believer from the path that he has chosen I would remind that when a single demon is exorcised from the life of an individual, seven others, each more destructive, wait to take up abode. If you save another from the clutches of a false prophet, who is the unredeemed redeemer? For as long as there is loneliness, as long as the difference between good and evil is a blur in our minds, as long as we feel unloved and incapable of loving, as long as our quest for personal significance is frustrated, the inner ear will strain to hear strange messengers, new gospels, whispers of hope. Listen well—whether you regard the promises as cruel hoaxes or as revelations of God. The cults cannot be ignored.

The cults are coming!

VIII. THE PEOPLES TEMPLE AND JONESTOWN

Thoughts on the Peoples Temple

My friend Tom Roberts is one of the lucky ones. He escaped the Peoples Temple. He is one of the luckiest of the lucky ones. His wife, children, in-laws, and grandchildren escaped with him. Only his son's beautiful wife was left behind to perish at Jonestown.

Tom's involvement began in 1973. He was a carpenter living in Modesto when he heard about Jim Jones. When he was invited to a service at a local high school he was prepared to dismiss Jones as another "holy roller." However, he was greatly impressed by the young preacher's gifts of "discernment" (telepathy) and healing, as well as by Jones' emphasis upon racial justice and care for the poor and needy. Tom and his family began traveling to Redwood Valley on a regular basis. The life of the community reaffirmed the preaching of Jones. Tom came to believe that the Peoples Temple truly represented a viable "apostolic socialism," a community united in love and service under the leadership of God's chosen prophet. As Tom recalls the message of "Father": "In every age God manifests himself in the life of an ideal community. Mankind is able to recognize that community because the miracles of the ministry of Jesus reappear in its life."

At a healing service in Redwood Valley, Jones raised a woman from the dead. In the next moment, he invited Tom to join "the Cause." Tom and his wife moved to Redwood Valley and were soon joined by their family and relatives. In short order, Tom was placed in charge of carpentry projects for the Peoples Temple. He and his wife, Sarah, graduated from the "periphery" (the Sunday-only worshipers) to the active membership. They attended Wednesday night "catharsis" meetings in which the verbal assaults on and humiliations of the "Family" members by Jones greatly troubled them. But Tom and Sarah assured themselves that there must be a reason for everything. After all, in all their spiritual wanderings they had never found any group so characterized by caring, love, and service. And no religious leader ever possessed such gifts of intuition and healing. "I know that Father faked many of the miracles," Tom admits today. "But I also know that many were real. He healed Sarah of cancer and could read my mind like an open book."

Three months after moving to Redwood Valley, Tom and Sarah were invited by Jones to join the "Planning Commission." They felt greatly honored by this opportunity to be part of the inner circle that ran things at the Peoples Temple. Their first meeting was a revelation and a nightmare! Jones bragged of his sexual experiences with both women and men in the group. His language was foul and crude. He openly claimed to be the father of John-John, the child of Grace Stoen. Jones disclosed to this core group that he had lived many previous lives: "When I was Moses, you were with me in the wilderness, and I led you safely out of slavery and death into the Promised Land. When I was Buddha, you were my followers, and I taught you to meditate upon me. When I was Mohammed, you sought after my teachings and served me with all your heart and being. When I was Jesus Christ, you were my disciples."

Hours passed as Jones reviled his followers for draining him of his sexual and emotional energy. Tom was stunned, nauseated, and enraged by the degeneracy of this man whom he had revered. He had believed so much in Jim Jones, and now he was destroyed—emotionally, spiritually, and psychologically. He felt totally betrayed. One thought governed his life: He had to get himself and his family out of that madhouse.

When the meeting finally ended at eight in the morning, Tom and Sarah were too embarrassed to look at anyone. They left as quickly as possible and headed for the trailer that was their home in Redwood Valley. They were surprised to see suitcases on the front step. Struggling to make his voice sound normal, Tom asked one of the workers who was loading the belongings into a truck, "Where are you going with our things?"

"Hi, Tom. Father asked me to get your children's clothes and help them get moved in with some other children their own age. You know how Father likes to get little ones educated, flowing and loving each other. I'm not sure where they are. You can find out though. Don't worry."

Tom and Sarah stared at each other like frenzied animals as their minds shared a single thought, "Oh, God, he has taken away our children!" The Roberts' waking nightmare continued for three years. The catharsis meetings got worse. Planning commission members were stripped naked, beaten, and forced to engage in sexual perversions. In the public meetings of members, children were beaten with a large wooden paddle or forced into a boxing ring where they were pummeled mercilessly by older children. Jones' public utterances became progressively more antigovernment. He claimed credit for the explosion of a munitions train. His sexual practices became increasingly more brutal and sadistic. He threatened dissidents and defectors with murder. All the while, his ministry to the sick, his healings, resurrections of the dead, and acts of mind-reading multiplied.

Finally Tom and Sarah's sense of terror overcame their need to believe, and they successfully plotted the simultaneous escape of all but one member of their large family from various parts of the Peoples Temple compound. During the two-year gap between his departure and the mass suicide-murder in Guyana, Tom continued to consult with Jones before making any important decision. He attempted to call the attention of the California attorney general's office to many illegal acts committed by Jones' followers while assuring Father that he remained a faithful disciple. Tom's mental confusion was mirrored by his personal life. His marriage of thirty years ended in divorce, and the business he started went bankrupt. Even now he believes that the power of Jim Jones reaches out from beyond the grave to bring disaster to those who once opposed him. For example, Tom claims that the murders of Mayor George Moscone and Supervisor Harvey Milk in San Francisco were preprogrammed by Jones, who long ago implanted a posthypnotic suggestion in the mind of their assassin, former Supervisor Dan White.

There is a dream that he and the Peoples Temple-Jonestown survivors have. They suddenly awake to find themselves at Jonestown, their life since the Peoples Temple a delusion. Jim Jones stands over them and has total control once again.

Was Jonestown a special case? Are there no lessons to be learned? What made the Peoples Temple work? How did this self-proclaimed god fasten his hold upon the bodies, minds, imaginations, and hopes of his followers? Totalistic groups cannot successfully make such high demands unless the leader commands a complete sacrifice of the followers' independent will. Remember the formula: Total submission produces total fulfillment. Jim Jones offered what all cult leaders offer: easy answers in return for total submission. Unless you respond fully, unthinkingly, without regret, without mental reservation, without hesitation, then you are unworthy to inherit the kingdom of God.

Recently I was speaking with an attractive twenty-year-old nursing student who was attracted to a high-demands cult group. Her friends in the group are telling her that the end is near and that she should sacrifice her family and career for the sake of the redemption of the human race. On the one hand, she is afraid that the group is right and that her present activities and plans are an impediment to her true calling. On the other hand, she is afraid that if she surrenders to the dictates of the group, fifty years from now she will realize that she has been a fool and has thrown away any chance of a productive life. It would be so much easier for her if someone like Jim Jones would settle her dilemma and tell her what to do. And if she places her life in the hands of such a charismatic leader, then her fate will only be as secure as the sanity of that leader. The one restraint on the demands of a cult leader is the leader's grasp of reality. To the self-appointed messiah, the world outside the group is evil—hostile, materialistic, unspiritual, depraved—in sum, godless. The founder perceives and represents the outside world to his disciple as the enemy waiting to be conquered for God, the domain of Satan eager to destroy the works of God. The leader sends forth his people as God's shock troops, his beachhead, his invasion force. The means justify the ends. Anything that will destroy the power of the foe is permitted—secrecy, threats, punishments, espionage, sabotage, mayhem, death, destruction. This is war, total and unconditional. The soldier of the perfect cause is instructed to neither ask nor grant quarter. The cultist expects the enmity of those whom he once loved. He expects that his friends, his mother and his father, his husband or wife, and even his own thoughts and memories will betray him.

The cult leader proclaims that "these are the last days. It is time to stand up and be counted. God is separating his sheep from Satan's goats. He who hesitates is lost. He who questions our great mission is a traitor." The "all or nothing" god of such groups has let loose "the fateful lightening of his terrible swift sword." The battlefield is no place for the tenderhearted, the humane, or the compassionate. The cultist believes unconditionally and irrevocably in the founder and his message. Hence, the only restraint resides in the inhibitions of the founder. If the founder fears the retaliation of agencies of social control, he will moderate his demands. If he feels he is beyond the laws of mankind but still grants grudging recognition of the power of the enemy, he may think before he acts. But if he believes totally in the divinity which has been bestowed upon him by his worshiping throng of followers or if he is convinced that the end of his ministry and mission is at hand, then no power can stay his hand. The metaphors of war through which the cult leader expresses his animosity toward the world and with which he justifies his call for obedience—these metaphors can readily become commands to attack, assault, beat, pillage, provoke, and even murder. The apocalyptic language that lends urgency to the founder's appeals can become self-fulfilling prophecy of Armageddon now!

The conviction that the cultist is totally right and others are completely wrong, that the former is chosen by God and the latter are condemned to eternal perdition, infuses the consciousness, the dreams, and the daily life of the true believer. It allows and encourages the cultist to lie, cheat, and steal. It mandates efforts to destroy families, to set husband against wife, to set child against mother. It leads to such moral atrocities as the covert evangelizing of young children, the destruction of self-choice in young adults, and the complete and final transformation of autonomous human beings into blindless automatons. Wanting to believe and needing to submit grant enormous power to the objects of our belief. If this power is unchecked, either by individual conscience or communal consensus, then each new convert is one more radioactive particle bringing the entire body ever nearer to critical mass.

Thoughts About the Dead in Guyana

In the weeks that followed the Jonestown massacre, I heard the horrors of the Peoples Temple recounted almost on a daily basis as I attempted to console escapees, defectors, and bereaved relatives. Somehow I managed to keep emotional distance between myself and the tragedy. And then, one rainy evening in March of 1978 as I drove across the San Mateo Bridge on my way home, I began thinking again about the dead in Jonestown. I reflected, somewhat heartlessly, that they all would have died anyway, sooner or later, and that had it not been for their slavish devotion these lives would probably have meant nothing. The dream of Jonestown had given them life and then had taken it from them.

Suddenly my mind shifted to the dead children, the three hundred incipient human stories that had been snuffed out. A week before, I had spent an evening with survivors and defectors viewing NBC video tape of the Ryan party's visit to Jonestown. We had stopped the tape frequently so that the names and identities of the children could be written down. I had never shed a tear for the fathers and mothers, the grandparents, the husbands and wives, the crafty and the outfoxed—Jonestown's big people. Jones twisted their arms and mangled their minds while drawing his strength from their abject weakness. I had never cried for them. But when I thought of three hundred little ones—"Dad's nursery," the temple's tomorrow that was never to be—when I thought of their deaths, I ached as though someone had just announced mine.

As I drove across the bay my hands tightened on the steering wheel, and I began to scream, "Sometime, somewhere, someone must accept responsibility!" If the god one worships and loves and serves—if this god deceives and defrauds, then one must own up and say that it is one's own fault—that one gave him the power to destroy. One accepts the blame. We get exactly what we deserve.

Perhaps it is better to sacrifice one's life to a false god than to live a life of shallow nothingness. How can we battle the false gods without the truth? How do we detect the counterfeit deities without the Deity? And if all gods are false, why bother toppling the Sun Myung Moons and the Moses Davids and their ilk? Maybe we should be thankful that Jones had only his hundreds and that the other cults have only stolen the minds of a few score thousand. What if something better comes along than these two-bit, hoodlum gods?

And at that moment I realized I was of two minds. On the one hand, I am the stuff of which cults are made. I am guilt-ridden and hungry for love but not always capable of giving love in return. I am dissatisfied with my self-pitying smallness. Part of me seems to pray: "Take my life, O great leader of some great cause. Take my life as if it were a checkbook. Spend me. Balance me. Replenish me. Cancel and annul my deficits. Assume my liabilities and to you shall all the credits and interest accrue. Amen."

Yet I am well aware that I am the stuff of which free men are made. My aspirations break the chains of sniveling cowardice. Let no man call me child or servant, for I am my own master. I bow in awe only before those noble souls who rule their own life.

It is all so simple. Let God be God. The life he has blessed me with is mine. The heart that confesses, "I have done this, I have made this life good or evil," is the only one that can resist the hoodlum gods.

Let God be God. The rediscovery of this truth has been the key to my post-Jonestown life and career. I will not walk with the credulous or the intolerant. There is no easy answer. All too often, God hides his smile and his frown. The clouds that have taken up his Son are thick and impenetrable.

"Let God be God," I tell my clients. "Do not worship the

rip-off gods of today. The hero you seek, the cause for which you would spend your life, is within you. It always has been and always will be. Love yourself for this, and you will always be loved."

As my thoughts returned to the bridge, the traffic, and the rain I looked ahead to the west where golden shafts of light filtered through the curtain of gray. In my mind's ear, I heard a Negro spiritual:

> I'm gonna walk this lonesome valley.
> I'm gonna walk it on my own.
> No one else can walk it for me.
> Gonna walk this lonesome valley on my own.

IX. FREEDOM COUNSELING CENTER—AN INNOVATIVE APPROACH

November 18, 1978. A date that forever changed the world's understanding of the word *cult*. The day on which the direction and purpose of my life were fundamentally and perhaps irrevocably altered.

Jonestown! The mass suicide-murder of an entire religious community of nearly one thousand. Who could in their wildest imaginings believe that more than nine hundred men, women, and children would allow—let alone enthusiastically embrace—their misguided messiah's command to join him in death!

The publication of the original edition of this book, *The Cults Are Coming,* destined me to a minor, peripheral role in the Jonestown disaster. And my attempts to assist the survivors and to interpret the Peoples Temple to the public led me to embark upon a new career as founder and director of

Freedom Counseling Center, a unique resource for families disrupted by cults.

When *The Cults Are Coming* appeared in mid-1978, I began to receive letters and phone calls from parents who had been driven to depression and despair by their sons and daughters' involvement in what they believed to be dangerous extremist groups. I tried to help them separate fact from fiction, legitimate concern from exaggerated terror. During the summer and early autumn, one group prompted the lion's share of these cult-related pleas for help.

This began when a local schoolteacher described to me a jungle concentration camp in Guyana in which her son was being held against his will. She told me of escapees' allegations of beatings, death threats, forced druggings, and murder. Her few radio-telephone conversations with her son proved to her that he was virtually a prisoner in Jim Jones' perverted paradise and that the young man was appealing to her to rescue him. It sounded to me as though this mother were allowing her protective instincts to run amok. When she concluded her story by telling me that she was attempting to hire a Rhodesian mercenary to head an armed expedition, I was sure that this lady's sanity had been severely strained by her maternal concern.

But Jonestown proved impossible to ignore. That summer, myriad stories appeared in the San Francisco newspapers and in California's *New West* magazine. Defectors from earlier enclaves in Ukiah (northern California) and in San Francisco were spreading chilling tales of violence, fraud, extortion, group humiliations, sexual perversions, and, above all, preparations for mass suicide. By early November, I had personally interviewed nearly twenty former members and knew for a certainty that Jonestown was a powder keg waiting for a spark.

The concerned relatives and former members had won the ear of my congressman, Leo Ryan, and he was about to embark on a fact-finding mission to Guyana. Naïvely believing that it would be of value to the Ryan party to have an experienced participative observer who could help cut through the expected public-relations circus that Jones would undoubtedly arrange at the enclave, I went to Ryan's San Mateo office and volunteered to join the expedition. By the time my offer reached Ryan he was embarking from JFK Airport in New York, and thus I lost my opportunity to become a footnote to history and gained a chance to aid the survivors of the Guyana disaster.

A month after Jonestown, I resigned as director of the Mental Health Association of San Mateo County and started a counseling service for "individuals and families disturbed by cults." The following month, I joined my efforts to those of several former members of the Peoples Temple in the development of the Human Freedom Center in Berkeley. After seven months of feeding, counseling, and housing Jonestown survivors as well as defectors from such other cult groups as the Unification Church, Divine Light Mission, the Hare Krishnas, Synanon, and Christ Family, I relocated near the San Francisco International Airport and began Freedom Counseling Center. Three years later the center continues to be America's only professional agency wholly dedicated to assisting individuals and families whose lives have been disturbed by cults, sects, communes, mass therapies (e.g., *est*, Lifespring), and other authoritarian groups.

In the months following the Jonestown massacre, cults received unprecedented media and governmental attention. Several nontraditional religious groups, particularly the Unification Church of Sun Myung Moon, were accused of brainwashing their members, destroying families, ruining careers, engaging in massive financial fraud, and preparing their members for fates similar to those suffered by the followers of Jim Jones. Parents who had never been overly concerned with the unusual religious beliefs and peculiar life-styles of their twenty-to-thirty-year-old offspring now became fearful, distressed, and often distraught. Deprogrammings multiplied.

Nontraditional groups, in turn, became more insecure and paranoid. Measures aimed at protecting members against the kidnappers and against the widely disseminated viewpoints of dissatisfied former members and other critics became more severe and restrictive. Scattered incidents of violence between deprogrammers and cult-security personnel were reported. A deprogrammer was threatened at knifepoint in Wisconsin. Another was fired upon in Virginia. Parents visiting their son at a Unification Church recruitment camp in California were assaulted by a number of men. An outbuilding at a Moonie recruitment center was firebombed. Cult members escaped from deprogrammings and brought law suits against their own parents. Parents and successfully deprogrammed cultists brought court actions against cults.

And much more severe than the few violent acts and the incessant legal wranglings were the post-Jonestown rhetorical barrages. First the anticult movement, a coalition of concerned parents, deprogrammers, and apostates from various nontraditional groups fired their salvos: "Brainwashing, violence, death pacts alleged!" Then the new religious movements and their allies, the first-amendment-civil-libertarian forces returned fire with accusations of intolerance, interference with religious liberties as well as atrocity stories of physical, psychological, and sexual violation of young adults by the vigilante deprogrammers.

In the midst of the cult-anticult wars of the late 1970s, Freedom Counseling Center was founded as a voice of moderation. While fully recognizing the dangers and threats of unchecked religious fanaticism, we are dedicated to noncoercive and effective means of assisting our clients. In other words, we know that there is a problem, and we believe that there are better ways than forcible deprogramming for dealing with it.

The Problem

What exactly is a cult? The term *cult* does not have a precise scientific meaning. When I speak of cults, I am referring to certain kinds of authoritarian religious movements that tend to disrupt the lives of involved followers. These movements share common characteristics.

A cult is a *nontraditional* religious group based upon the teachings of an *authoritarian* leader. A single individual is the sole source of what the group believes and of the rules that govern daily behavior.

A cult is a *highly structured, strictly disciplined* group that demands the total time, dedication, and resources of its members. Further, a cult has the means to enforce its demands via humiliation, punishment, beatings, death threats, or even murder. Usually, embarrassing a wayward member before his peers or making him feel guilty about his lack of dedication is sufficient.

A cult sees itself as the *only possessor of truth* and regards those outside the cult as unsaved, unenlightened, unspiritual, and hostile to the truth.

Primary cult activities are *new-member recruitment and fund-raising*. Cults may claim all manner of social-betterment and educational activities, but in most cases these turn out to be forms of evangelism or raising funds for the group itself.

Cult initiation techniques are frequently based upon *deception* and *psychological coercion*. Potential recruits are misled about the true identity of the group and about the true purpose of its activities. They are brought into totally controlled, secluded environments where they are subjected to the bombardment of strange new ideas, the constant pressure of peer approval or rejection, physical exhaustion, unusual or poor diet, and the induction of phobias concerning their lives, work, friends, and family.

Most cults employ systematic forms of *consciousness-altering practices* (chanting, speaking in tongues, listening to hours of boring tape recordings, recitation of memorized material, etc.) that make individuals suggestible to group dictates and group control rather than to self-determination.

Money is often obtained under *false pretenses*.

Members of cults are encouraged to *cut off communications* with family members and friends.

Cultists allow the group leader to make *important decisions* concerning career and marriage for them.

In many instances, cult members give their possessions and earnings to the group and, in turn, become *totally dependent* on the group.

What family and close friends witness is the adoption by a child or friend of a new identity and the repudiation of manifestations of former life, including contacts with relatives and loved ones. Bewildered by sudden and drastic personality changes, concerned relatives and friends desperately seek assistance. However, they soon discover that this problem lies outside the scope of traditional counseling services. Where can they turn for help? Freedom Counseling Center provides sensitive and appropriate services to individuals and families whose lives have been disrupted by cults and other nontraditional groups. The center has assisted over five hundred families throughout the world. It is a nonprofit public-benefit corporation with a dedicated staff of professionals and consultants who are specialists in the new field of cult-related counseling. The staff includes mental health practitioners, experts in religious experience, and former members of a variety of authoritarian groups.

One Solution

What is needed for counseling families and individuals involved with cults is an approach that respects the integrity of each client, supports genuine spiritual aspirations, and is noncoercive. The center provides such a service. It also cooperates fully with clergy, law enforcement officers, and other involved professionals. The goal is not to convert clients to any philosophy but to support their return to autonomy and adulthood.

The simplest way of describing the kind of approach that helps families and former cult members return to normal living is to relate a typical case handled by the Freedom Counseling Center. It is a composite of numerous actual cases with which the center has dealt during the past four years.

A mother and father from New Mexico phone the center concerning their son who has been missing for four months. Our "subject" is twenty-two years of age, a college dropout who has been backpacking through California, Oregon, and Washington State. In the months prior to his disappearance he has often alarmed his parents with stories of psychedelic drug experimentation and strange dieting-fasting practices. Just before phoning me, they have received a letter from him with a New York City postmark. The letter is filled with talk about a "new age community," that is preparing the way for the imminent return of the Messiah by living together communally and demonstrating selfless love. The parents ask us to help them by locating their son, providing them with data about the group he has joined, and assisting them in the development of a strategy for encouraging the young man to accept responsibility for his own life.

The catchphrases in the letter tell me that our subject has joined a cult group that maintains recruitment- and training-centers in New York City and Allentown, Pennsylvania. The family and I fly to New York City where, under my guidance, they make contact with the leadership at the group's headquarters in Manhattan. I prepare them for the various dodges and evasions they will face, and by following our game plan, they locate their son and make arrangements to see him the following day. Overnight the group moves him from Manhattan and tells the parents that he has left of his own free will because he does not want to see them and that they do not know his present whereabouts. We rent a car and drive to Allentown, and the parents repeat the process of the previous day, parrying the lies and evasions of the group until their son is produced.